A Town Called Sutherland Springs

Faith and Heroism Through Tragedy

Stephen Willeford

and

Rachel Howe

A Town Called Sutherland Springs

Original Title:

"A Town Called Sutherland Springs:

Faith and Heroism Through Tragedy"

Copyright © Stephen Willeford & Rachel Howe, 2023

Cover, Photo credit:

"Daniel Contreras, New Dirt Studios"

Stephen Willeford & Rachel Howe

The town of Sutherland Springs lived in quiet obscurity, until a madman entered the First Baptist Church on November 5th, 2017. This book recounts the harrowing story of those who lived through that day, witnessed terrible evil, and rose to face it. Hope can be found in their faith, heroism, and actions, and in the overwhelming presence of God.

"Sometimes a thunderbolt, as men call it, will shoot from a clear sky; and sometimes into the midst of a peaceful family, or a yet quieter individuality, without warning of gathered storm above, or lightest tremble of earthquake beneath, will fall a terrible fact, and from the moment everything is changed. That family or that life is no more what it was - probably nevermore can be what it was. Better it ought to be, worse it may be - which, depends upon itself. But its spiritual weather is altered. The air is thick with cloud, and cannot weep itself clear. There may come a gorgeous sunset though." -George MacDonald, *Thomas Wingfold, Curate,* Chapter 21

A Town Called Sutherland Springs

For the survivors, first responders, and all those who showed incredible strength, courage, and faith throughout this tragedy. Thank you for sharing with us. Thank you for shining your light in a dark and twisted world.

Isaiah 43:2

Stephen Willeford & Rachel Howe

Contents

Forward 6

Introduction 8

Chapter One: A Wolf at the Door 11

Chapter Two: Evil Enters Sanctuary 32

Chapter Three: A Call to Arms 49

Chapter Four: Exchanging Fire 70

Chapter Five: Triage 91

Chapter Six: Gunpowder and Blood 116

Chapter Seven: The Longest Seven Minutes 142

Chapter Eight: A Remnant 169

Chapter Nine: Finding Hope 191

Afterword 216

About the Authors 218

Acknowledgments 220

Forward

Everyone thinks that they will be the hero. But reality doesn't always meet our dreams when the need arises. As we have seen from the mass murders at the Parkland or Uvalde schools, even police officers, who are paid to run towards danger, are once in a while afraid to confront the murderers. There were 376 law enforcement officers in Uvalde, and some officers waited as long as one hour and fourteen minutes while that monster murdered 21 people before the police entered the classroom. Officers stood by At Parkland, then Broward County Deputy Scot Peterson hid rather than confront the murderer while he slaughtered 17 people. Only God knows how many lives could have been saved through fast action.

If you want to know what type of person runs towards bullets to save lives, read this book, and you will learn the kind of person Stephen Willeford is. Steve grabbed his AR-15 and, in his bare feet, ran towards the monster who was murdering parishioners at the Baptist Church in Sutherland Springs.

Stephen not only confronted the murderer and halted his attack, but when the murderer fled the scene, Stephen, with the help of another person, chased after him.

Stephen Willeford & Rachel Howe

Stephen told the news media that he was "scared to death" and "terrified" while he responded to the attack. But that is what real heroes do. He did it despite being afraid.

But Stephen answers to a higher authority who he knows will hold him accountable. In this book, you will learn the values of faith and honor that make a person like Stephen who he is.

The news media would like to pretend that heroes like Stephen don't exist. And just a tiny fraction of the news coverage about the church shooting mentions Steve's role in stopping the attack. Yet, Stephen is one of those rare examples who at least gets some media coverage. From 2020 to February 15, 2023, the Crime Prevention Research Center that I head has compiled a list of 37 instances where police have said that people legally carrying guns have stopped what otherwise would have been a mass public shooting. Indeed, over 60 percent of the active shooting attacks from 2014 to 2022 where people were legally able to carry guns have seen legally armed civilians stop attacks. In places from restaurants to malls to city streets, Americans legally carrying concealed handguns keep stopping active and mass public shootings, but they almost always receive only local news coverage.

John R. Lott, Jr.

President, Crime Prevention Research Center

Author, "More Guns, Less Crime"

Introduction

Most of my life I've lived in this tiny town — a town where you can see the stars. A town where everyone is friendly because everyone is family. A town where anyone would give you the shirt off their back if you asked for it.

When I tell people where I live, it is inevitably followed by one specific question: "Where is that?!"

I always explain that it is a quiet little town centered in the middle of nowhere. Close enough to the city to not be too remote and far enough away to be peaceful. I always mention that we are composed of two gas stations, a post office, a handful of houses, and a little Baptist Church. The people who ask where I live inevitably forget moments later. Because what is there to remember about a little town like that?

It pains me that Sutherland Springs has now been immortalized in history for the horrific events at its little Baptist Church. The church, which is full of such Godly, friendly, beautiful people is the center and soul of our town. It pains me every time I hear "Sutherland Springs" come out of the lips of a politician, a news anchor, or an ignorant celebrity. They don't know us. They don't understand what Sutherland Springs is. It breaks my heart that my little town — once so easily forgotten — is now nationally known as the location of the worst church massacre in American history, and the worst mass killing in Texas modern times. I hate it that the people I love, the town I'm raising my children in, is stained with such a horrific moniker.

I refuse to give that evil man any victory over my town and its future. I refuse to let him change us, stain us. So let me tell you what we should be remembered for.

We should be remembered for the nurse who attended to members of her congregation even as she herself bled from a gunshot wound.

We should be remembered for the mother who died shielding her child from a hail of bullets.

We should be remembered for the man with medical training who rushed into the church and started pulling people out as soon as the killer left.

We should be remembered for the neighbor who cradled a little girl, shivering in shock, and kept her awake while wiping tears from her own eyes.

We should be remembered for the neighbors who brought water, towels, helping hands, prayers, and comfort to those who survived.

We should be remembered for the neighbor who ran to the church barefoot, with his gun, because his family needed him — and the stranger who let him into his truck to chase down the monster.

We should be remembered for the words of hope brought by the pastor and his wife, both of whom had suffered unimaginable loss. They praised God for his goodness and begged the community to trust in His plan.

A Town Called Sutherland Springs

The names of these heroes, these neighbors, these community members aren't what is important. Because this is our community — they are our soul. This is all of us. This is what we all did and continue to do.

This is Sutherland Springs. We are not victims. We are survivors. We are faithful. We are family. We are more than the media understands, more than the pathetic celebrities pushing their selfish agendas will ever fathom. We are strong. And we will pull through this.

Don't remember us for the killer's evil.

Remember us for who we are — the family of Sutherland Springs.

Stephen Willeford & Rachel Howe

Chapter One: A Wolf at the Door

My name is Stephen Willeford. I am an ordinary, Texas man. I am no more remarkable than any other average citizen, other than how remarkably blessed I am. I am married to a beautiful woman and have three kids who are now starting families of their own.

I have been a blue-collar worker all my life. There is something satisfying about working with your hands, committing a day to getting something accomplished that you can physically see. After dabbling in farming and oil field work, I ended up going to school and becoming a Plumber with the Local 142 Plumbers and Pipefitters Union in San Antonio, Texas. I did commercial construction jobs — jobs that required full days in blazing heat or random cold snaps. My job required me to climb around in rafters, or under buildings hauling and fitting heavy pipes, laying plans that were often scrapped, doubling back when something went wrong, and moving on once the job was completed. Construction was rough, as rough and hardened as the people who chose this line of work. I made many life-long friends at the Union, and always enjoyed conversations with them while working or sitting around the job site for lunch.

A Town Called Sutherland Springs

It was during one such work day, during a seemingly normal lunch break many years ago, that I had a conversation which I would remember for the rest of my life.

I don't remember the job site. There were so many over the years that they all begin to blur together. It was all the same work, with many of the same people, and after years and years they all meld into one with the imperfection of human memory. I do, however, remember Arturo.

Arturo was the Project Manager of the site. He had been sitting close to my apprentice and I as we talked about our weekend plans. He was silent for the most part, until our conversation pushed him over the edge.

I had been telling an apprentice about my weekend. That particular weekend, my friends and family and I had participated in a shooting competition. I was in the middle of describing the different drills we were tested on — odd drills like diapering a baby doll, picking it up, and shooting with one hand as you cradled the doll in the other, or shooting with your non-dominant hand- or shooting at bowling pins with the goal of only leaving the red ones standing.

I guess this was what pushed Art over the edge. He and I disagreed about a lot of things, guns being foremost.

"What is the purpose of these drills?" he interrupted, letting his skepticism creep into his voice, most likely unintentionally.

I turned to him, used to his confrontational tone. "For practice. For fun. But also, to prepare us for a worst-case scenario," I responded.

Arturo laughed. "As if anything could prepare you for that. All your drills, all your practice won't mean anything in the face of an active shooter situation. You'd probably be so scared you'd freeze up and pee your pants."

I smiled at him and shrugged. "You may be right. I might do those things. I don't know. Hopefully, I'll never have to find out."

"But-" I continued, "You practice martial arts, Arturo, and spend hours learning different forms, and moving from belt to belt. You practice all that discipline to hone your skills, to make sure if you are ever attacked, your reaction is immediate, and out of habit, don't you?"

Arturo was silent for a moment. "That's different," he said. "It's karate, not a shooter."

"It's not different," I told him. "I'm doing the same thing. And you may be right, I may freeze up in fear, and hide. I don't know. I will probably never know. But hopefully, if a terrible situation ever does occur, I will be the kind of man who is capable, in training, spirit, and mindset to protect someone else. God willing, I will have the courage to stand up, be a man, and stop evil, if I ever have the misfortune to see it. Only time will tell," I concluded.

"Like that would ever happen," Arturo smirked.

It wasn't an unusual thing to say or think. No one ever expects to be thrust into that kind of situation. Those things happen to other people, not to you. Not to your family. Not in your town, or neighborhood. Even so, I remember looking at him, serious for a moment, my smile fading.

A Town Called Sutherland Springs

"You just never know," I told him, turning back to my lunch.

* * *

Church was always central to my life, even when I was a child. I grew up on a dairy farm. My mornings were full of chores such as milking and caring for the cows, until the morning was long spent. Before I could leave for school, my brother Delbert and I had a list of things we had to accomplish- except on Sundays. On Sundays our parents handled the chores by themselves, while Mr. and Mrs. Goss picked us up early in the morning and drove us to church.

I can still remember crawling up into Mr. Goss' large four-door car. The seats were so huge that my legs couldn't reach the floor and would instead hang out in open air over the front. Every time we hit a bump, the car would bounce uncontrollably, and my brother and I would jostle around in the back seat. The trip to Stockdale required many dirt roads, including our own. It was always quite a ride.

No matter how much work had to be done in the mornings, Mom and Dad always made it very clear to us: God came first. Chores could be done later. So, as we sat in Bible class, Mom and Dad would quickly finish up the morning chores before joining us at church for worship service.

My wife and I always made sure to prioritize church in our children's lives, as my parents did. We would drive an hour into town every Sunday so our children could attend a church youth group that they loved.

Stephen Willeford & Rachel Howe

After our kids graduated high school, my wife and I continued going to church in San Antonio, but for some reason, it didn't quite fit anymore. We drifted for a while, struggling to find a new church home. Every time we visited a church, it felt like just that- visiting. Despite this struggle, we still went to church as often as we could.

Except one Sunday, on November 5th, 2017. I had started a new job. After over thirty years working in the local union as a plumber, I had finally earned my retirement, and now worked maintenance at University Hospital in San Antonio. Once every six weeks, for an entire week, I was on call for emergency maintenance. If there was a leak, a clogged sink, or another major problem with the plumbing, I would be called in to handle it at any time of the day or night. Because I started on call Monday, and because of our struggle to find a home church, I stayed home that morning, trying to get a little rest before the inevitable scream of my pager.

So, I slept in, while my wife, Pam got up to work on a house that my daughter and her husband were building. Little did I know that rest was not intended for me on this particular Sunday.

* * *

Julie Workman wasn't going to go to church. Pastor Frank was out of town. Her son was attending church and could lead worship. She didn't always have to go and sing in the worship team. They could have a service without her, right?

Instead, she would stay home with her husband. She would have a cup of coffee and sit on the porch. She would feed the cows, and just relax. It wouldn't be a big deal if she didn't go for one sermon.

As Julie climbed out of bed and made her way to the bathroom, she could hear a question, resounding clearly in her mind.

Julie, why do you go to church?

She ignored the question. She was going to stay home. She was going to relax.

As Julie washed the sleep from her eyes, and began to brush her teeth, she heard the voice again.

Why do you go to church? It asked.

No, she thought, firmly, looking in the mirror. Not today. I am tired today. I don't have to go every week.

As she entered her closet, rifling through her clothes preparing to get dressed, she heard the question a third time. This time it was more strict, more commanding.

Why do you go to church?

She sighed, catching her reflection in the mirror, her green eyes relenting. "Ok, God," she said aloud, knowing she couldn't deny him three times. "I'm no Peter. I get it."

Julie traded her everyday clothes for a new black dress, with pink and red flowers on it. She would go to church today. Church was her family. It was a place to go to worship God. She shouldn't just skip. No matter how tired she was.

✹ ✹ ✹

It was the end of daylight savings time. Everyone's clocks were messed up. Julie, Kris, and Bob Corrigan ribbed the church members who arrived, joking with those who didn't reset their clocks and dragged themselves in a full hour early.

There was a lot of eye-rolling and laughter, as was usual with the worship team. The small chapel was always filled with laughter. The members knew each other so well, they were as close as a family.

They were family.

As the three members of the worship team practiced for service that morning, a new couple entered through the large, double doors and made their way across the maroon carpet. Together, they silently settled into one of the pews toward the back.

"There is a Bible study in the fellowship hall," Julie told them, giving directions to the building. "If you wanted to go join everyone else."

The wife smiled with kind, brown eyes. "We would like to just listen to you practice, if that's ok."

Practice continued as usual until around 10:30, when Bible study ended, and members began to slowly file into the chapel. They talked, laughed, hugged, and shook hands. Little children ran around, hugging the knees of adults, bumping, and weaving through legs.

Five-year-old Brooke Ward ran over to the front of the church, and wrapped her little arms around Julie's legs, burying her face in the skirt of her dress. Brooke was wearing a Cinderella dress, the poofy, sparkling skirt billowing out around her as she twirled through the crowd. Julie wrapped the little girl in her arms. Brooke always gave the sweetest, and sometimes the most wild hugs.

Although church service technically started at eleven, this was a Baptist Church in South Texas. They never started on time. There was too much family to hug. Too many hands to shake. Too much catching up to do. So, as usual, ten or so minutes late, Julie's son Kris stood up at the front of the church, guitar in hand, and began the welcome song with Bob. Julie joined at the front, and the church began to sing, still milling about and hugging family and friends.

Have you been to Jesus for the cleansing power?
Are you washed in the blood of the lamb?
Are you fully trusting in His grace this hour?
Are you washed in the blood of the lamb?

People sang as they settled into their pews, still greeting their neighbors, the occasional bubble of laughter breaking out. The chorus of the church rose, imperfect and beautiful.

Are you washed in the blood,
In the soul cleansing blood of the lamb?
Are your garments spotless? Are they white as snow?
Are you washed in the blood of the lamb?

Brooke joined Julie on the stage, dancing around with wild joy, her Cinderella skirt spinning around her in gauzy waves.

Lay aside the garments that are stained with sin,
And be washed in the blood of the lamb.

Stephen Willeford & Rachel Howe

There's a fountain flowing for the soul unclean,

O, be washed in the blood of the lamb.

Julie watched Brooke spin, faster and faster at the front of the stage, reveling in the little girl's exuberance.

Are you washed in the blood,

In the soul-cleansing blood of the lamb?

Are your garments spotless? Are they white as snow?

Are you washed in the blood of the lamb?[1]

As the song ended, Brooke's smiling mother, Joann, beckoned for her little girl to return to her seat. Brooke bounded away, golden hair shining as she skipped to join her mother in the pew.

※ ※ ※

Robert Scott met Karen in North Carolina, at Seymour Johnson Air Force Base. Scott had just returned from Okinawa, Japan. Karen was working in the personnel office and handled his paperwork. They hit it off almost instantly. Robert- or "Scotty", as everyone called him - was loud, boisterous, and playful. Karen was quiet, more reserved, and cared deeply for people. Like opposite sides of a magnet, they were drawn to each other. They balanced each other out perfectly.

On August 3rd, 1985, Scotty and Karen got married. Together they had three children: Martina, Cara, and Brandon. Service was essential to both of them- Karen spent nine and a

---

[1] Elisha Hoffman "Are you Washed in the Blood", 1878

half years in the military, and then joined the National Guard, while Scotty served for eleven years. Their time spent in the military was a reflection of their life philosophy. They lived to help other people. Both deeply cared for people and were known for collecting strays. It was not unusual for them to have random military members they had just met over for family celebrations- Scotty could never stomach the idea of someone spending a holiday alone. Besides, the noise never bothered him.

They would give everything they had to people who needed help, and often did things in secret without taking any credit.

As a married couple, the two were spontaneous and adventurous. One day, their son Brandon came home from school and found the cord to the phone leading to the closet. Scotty and Karen were inside hiding behind the coats, on the phone with an airline, booking flights for a special trip. Later that day, they told their three children to pack a bag, and drove them to the airport. Despite protests and pleading for more information, Scotty and Karen kept their secrets until they boarded the plane as a family- set on a surprise family vacation to Hawaii for Thanksgiving. This was typical behavior for them. The world held adventure, and Scotty and Karen were determined to spend as much time soaking it up as they could. They loved to spend time outdoors, and they loved to camp.

Karen owned a 2008 Honda Goldwing motorcycle, and sometimes, she'd shove Scotty (who was the motorcycle operator) out the door for their own adventure. They loved to go riding around Texas on the weekends, or sometimes on longer trips to New Mexico or Big Bend. They would go sightseeing along the way, camp, and soak in the sunshine and fresh air.

Scotty had a dry sense of humor, a unique laugh that had a way of spreading, and a love for practical jokes. When his kids were young, he would hide behind doors or in closets wearing a monkey mask, waiting for the perfect moment to jump out and scare them. Sometimes, he would aim his jokes at Karen, and the kids would hear her indignant scream of "SCOTTY!!!" echoing across the house, followed by a frustrated slap to the shoulder. His humor often baffled Karen, who was more serious and stoic.

Despite Karen's stoicism, she was deeply caring, and fierce. She had a core of unshakeable opinions that she solidly stuck to. She was devoted to her family, to her career, and to her church in Maryland. She was often seen carrying her Bible, a pen, and a highlighter. She came to faith later in life, and seemed like she was trying to make up for lost time by discovering as much as she could within the thin pages of her Bible.

When Scotty moved to Sutherland Springs ahead of Karen to prepare their home for her arrival, one of the first things he did was to find a church.

They chose Sutherland Springs together, because it was close to Karen's new job. She would be stationed at Randolph Brooks Air Force Base, but they wanted the feel of

A Town Called Sutherland Springs

a small town, and they wanted land so they could live a country lifestyle. A church home was incredibly important to both of them.

Scotty was excited to show Karen the First Baptist Church in Sutherland Springs. He knew that she would love it. She had only been in Texas for a few days that Sunday morning, when they entered the double doors of the church early and listened to the band from their seats in the back pew. They had only just reunited after spending some time in different states due to Karen's career, and some prolonged health battles, requiring Scotty to move for treatment. They were always happier when they were together. When apart, they would spend hours on the phone, catching up, listening to the sound of each other's voices. Praying together. Looking forward to the day when they would be reunited on their farm in Sutherland Springs.

They were visitors at the church that day as they entered into the gates of heaven hand in hand, reunited with each other at last, and finally seeing the God that they both fiercely loved.

✳ ✳ ✳

Karla Holcombe stood at the pulpit, making Sunday morning announcements. She was applauding the volunteers for the Fall Festival. It had been a huge success. Attendance had been fantastic. A special shout out was given to Julie, who had come dressed as a hospital patient. A picture of the outfit was shown on the screen, making the whole congregation break out in scattered laughter.

Julie had gone all out. She had worn a hospital gown, with an IV taped to her arm, with a bag of what looked like blood. She had done her makeup to look exhausted, with stitches and bandages all over her. She even wore flesh-toned leggings with a giant pair of red granny panties underneath the gown, making it look like she was flashing her undergarments to whomever walked behind her. Everyone joked that she looked as though she had been hit by a train. They had tied it into a Biblical lesson, though. Don't let life take you unawares. You never know when life could hit you like a train. Karla presented Julie with a small, silly little trophy to reward her for the costume.

It was as she was making her way back to the second pew, where she usually sat during service, when she heard it. Short, loud bursts cracking through the air outside.

Fireworks? As Julie sat on the pew, her eyes immediately searched for the congregation's teenage boys. Was this a prank, or part of service?

When she spotted two of them in the pews, looking around just as she was, she knew it was something different.

Noises like this weren't entirely out of the ordinary in their small, country church. Just last week, Pastor Frank had ridden his Harley Davidson into the sanctuary. They were known to sometimes use visual or auditory props in service.

A Town Called Sutherland Springs

She glanced at Bryan Holcombe, who was doing the lesson today. What was he doing?

Bryan looked just as confused as she did. Ok, something is definitely wrong.

With a loud pop, the globe on the fan above Julie's head burst, raining glass down. It tinkled and scattered across the pew, falling onto the maroon carpet, as the loud cracks from outside continued. It was then that she recognized the sound. Bullets.

Julie raised her hands above her head instinctively, protecting herself from the raining glass. Wait, bullets? It couldn't be.

"I'm hit!" a scream rose from the back of the church. "I'm hit!"

It was Haley Krueger. 16-year-old Haley, who just that morning had helped prepare breakfast for the church.

Haley's words broke Julie's denial. Gunfire. The noise was gunfire.

* * *

Haley Krueger was a vivacious 16-year-old. Although she seemed quiet upon first meeting, it didn't take much to coax the girl out of her shell. Then, like a vibrant, colorful butterfly, she would spring from her cocoon, and spread her wings. Once unleashed, Haley was never quiet again. Her personality was as beautiful as her bright, sky-blue eyes and loving smile. She laughed often and cared deeply for everyone.

Like many teenage girls, Haley had a penchant for fashion. She had her own unique brand, however, which could be easily recognized. She loved bows- the bigger and brighter, the better. Haley would not leave the house without one fixed in her long brown hair. Her mother, Charlene, would laugh when Haley came out of her room, often three times a day with a different outfit. She had to find the perfect thing to wear every day and would not be happy unless her outfit was just right. Oftentimes, Haley and her older sister, Camey, would do each other's makeup, and the house would be filled with delightful squeals as innocent makeovers turned into ridiculously painted faces. Haley loved to laugh.

Haley was her mother's sidekick. They did everything together. In preparation for the Rock N' Roll Marathon, the two would take long walks in the La Vernia city park every evening. As the sun set, lighting the sky in brilliant pinks and oranges, they would talk about their day, laugh, and sweat.

Whenever they were in the car, Haley would grab Charlene's phone and be her own personal DJ. She would play selections from Miley Cyrus and Taylor Swift- but always started with Dylan Scott, who was by far her favorite. She loved the song "My Girl" and would sing it as they drove down the road, blaring music, and telling her mom all about her favorite songs.

The first time Charlene introduced Haley to her boyfriend, it was a school day. Haley had just hopped off the bus and flown into the living room to find Lance sitting on the couch. Charlene introduced him to her daughter. Haley broke into one of her famous, room-brightening smiles and pointed at the two of them.

"I'll be right back!" she exclaimed, hiking her backpack up higher.

With that, she spun on her heel, and flounced into her room. Lance and Charlene looked at each other, confused, as Haley came whirling back, her Bible clutched tightly in her hands.

"You need JESUS!" She proclaimed, skipping up to him and smacking the Bible into his stomach with a solid whump.

Then, Haley pranced off back to her room, her wild laughter following her.

Haley's faith in God was strong, and she was never afraid to share it with anyone who would listen. She cared deeply for people and wanted desperately to make the world a better place. From the time she was young, she wanted to be a NICU nurse. She planned to attend Galen School of Nursing and dedicate her life to taking care of the innocent. She was terrific with kids, and always seemed to know instinctively how to comfort a child, or cheer one up. It was not unusual to see Haley slipping around the house with socks on, falling dramatically, crashing into things and flopping down wildly on chairs just to get a chuckle out of Mikayla and Maverick, a few young family friends. There were no limits to the amount of things Haley would do to make a child, or anyone else happy.

Haley had a gentle, mothering nature. She loved to take care of people, and make sure they had everything they needed. No one knew this more than Haley's little brother, Landon. He was a year younger than her and has autism. Haley didn't treat him any differently though. She would set aside time to make sure they could go outside and play catch. She would walk with him to classes, to make sure he got there ok, and check on him throughout the day. She would check to be sure he took his medicine, to see how his day was going, and be there for him whenever he needed anything. Even though Haley still occasionally got into squabbles and arguments with her three siblings, no one could deny that she loved them fiercely.

Haley always drank Dr Pepper and was prone to hoarding the drink beneath her bed. She loved to binge watch Heartland or Grey's Anatomy with her mother. She wanted to visit Canada, learn to ride horses, and take another trip to a NASCAR race with her family. Her faith in God and joyful spirit carried her through life, igniting in her a desire to help whomever she could and change the world.

In the short time that Haley graced this world, she impacted many lives and brought laughter and joy wherever she went. Though some of her plans were left undone, Haley without a doubt did change those around her, and make the world a better place. She entered the kingdom of Heaven on November 5, surrounded by friends, family, and loved ones.

A Town Called Sutherland Springs

She had been a member of First Baptist Church of Sutherland Springs for seven years.

* * *

Sarah Slavin had been planning on attending First Baptist Church of Floresville that morning but had inexplicably fallen asleep after her alarm roused her. Tired from the day-to-day stresses of motherhood, Sarah's bed had been too inviting, too warm, and too comfortable to abandon so early.

When she woke quite a while later, groggy and confused, she knew it was too late to make the service in Floresville. Instead, she leapt out of bed and hastily readied herself, rushing along her two-year-old daughter, Elene, in the process. As it took her longer and longer to get out of the door, dressing her daughter, cramming shoes on her feet, gathering her own clothes and belongings, Sarah knew there would be no getting around being late today. When she finally loaded her daughter into her vehicle and climbed into the front, Sarah glanced briefly at the clock. She would not only be late to church in Sutherland Springs today, but late by at least half an hour. Oh, well. At least she would be there.

As she began to drive down the dirt road, her mind filled with the kind of common, everyday worries that young mothers deal with, Sarah felt an overwhelming presence in the car with her. So startling and tangible was the feeling that Sarah found herself looking to her right, to the empty passenger seat, sure someone had materialized next to her.

She was surprised to find herself and Elene alone in the car, although the logical center of her brain told her they were.

The presence itself was overwhelming: it brought to her a kind of peace she had never known before. A peace so euphoric and whole that tears came to her eyes. In that moment, she knew everything was going to be ok. All the anxieties she had been agonizing over her entire life, and all her insecurities were washed away in the presence of that all-encompassing love.

You are going to be ok, it seemed to be telling her. Elene is going to be ok. I will keep her safe. I will protect her.

All her life, Sarah had heard her mother, Karla, describe her interactions with God. All her life, she had listened in wishful skepticism as her mother recounted her daily experiences with the Holy Spirit. It wasn't as if Sarah didn't believe in God. She did, in a theoretical sense. She attended church. She read the Bible. She prayed. But it was never as real as she wanted it to be. She heard the testimonies of those in her life who had felt God's presence with a kind of wistful jealousy. She wanted to believe as strongly in His existence as they did. She wanted to experience the unerring faith of her mother. Until that moment in her car, Sarah had not.

But in that moment, Sarah knew with unshakable certainty that God was real. She knew His presence was beside her, and all around her. It was like someone was in the car with her- someone who loved her more than anyone else in the entire world, someone who knew her down to the core of her being. The knowledge was so strong, Sarah almost pulled into her grandparents' driveway as she drove past, to run inside and tell them. She couldn't keep news like this to herself. She had to tell someone.

But she was already running late to church, and right now she wanted to be there more than she had in a long time. Smiling, euphoric, and filled with the kind of peace that truly passed all understanding, Sarah pulled onto the highway and continued on to church, where she would tell her parents and family what she had experienced.

* * *

Bob and Shani Corrigan were married for 32 years. They were vibrant, joyful people, whose laughter always came easily, and whose love for Christ shone through every action. Bob served for thirty years in the United States Air Force, ending his career as Chief Master Sergeant in 2015. Once retired, he and Shani moved back to Floresville, Texas, and returned to the First Baptist Church of Sutherland Springs, where they had been members while stationed in San Antonio.

Bob loved music and song writing. He played the guitar and sang in the church worship team. He was a caring man, with a deep passion for all the people he met. His childlike spirit and joyful attitude won people over quickly, and his strong faith and caring nature made those around him feel important.

Shani was known for her exuberance. Most of the time, she was quiet and observant, but she laughed often and, like her husband, had a beautiful childlike side. She came alive when she told stories: her wild hand gestures, commanding voice, and sense of humor captivating an audience with ease. Like her husband, Shani loved to sing, and often lent her beautiful voice to Sunday morning worship services.

Bob and Shani were high school sweethearts. Together, they had three children. They loved their church, and the people in it desperately.

Shani had just volunteered to take over the kitchen on Thursday nights. Every Thursday, the church hosted dinner and a Bible study. The week before the tragedy, they had announced the need for someone to take over the kitchen during the morning Ladies' Bible study.

"Ok, God, FINE!" Shani announced dramatically, producing chuckles from her church family. It had been gnawing on her heart to help more. Not one to miss a chance to make people laugh, Shani dramatically gave in to her calling and volunteered to take over.

They had been family members of the First Baptist Church in Sutherland Springs for twelve years when they entered the kingdom of God, together, as they had been for most of their lives.

Chapter Two: Evil Enters Sanctuary

By all accounts, it was a normal Sunday. Stephanie was skipping church today. One of her best friends was getting married, and she had some things to wrap up around the house before she attended the wedding. She also had to wait for her fiancé to get off work so they could drive into town together.

The dishes were the first item on the agenda. She stood in the kitchen, arms deep to the elbows in soapy, warm water. The dishes were clacking together as the TV show streaming on her phone warbled in the background, canned laughter from a laugh track playing between jokes.

She was on autopilot. The sooner she finished the dishes, the sooner she could get ready for the wedding. She already had the dress she was going to wear picked out, hanging on the folding door of her closet.

That is when she heard the noise. Her hands stilled in the murky water, as she looked up, peering through the curtains masking the window above the sink.

Fireworks?

As the noise continued, she knew she was wrong. It was a sound with which she was familiar. Years of Sunday afternoons on the shooting range as a kid had ingrained the sound into her brain.

Gunfire.

Brush obscured anything past the confines of the metal link fence of the backyard, and overgrown trees blocked her view of the street. She didn't know where it was coming from — only the direction. It was in the direction of the church.

Leaving her phone behind, Stephanie turned and ran down the hall, spattering droplets of dish water across the tile as she went.

* * *

For her sixteenth birthday Stephanie had decided to have a giant camping trip. It was a huge party. Her dad, Stephen, had pulled out his modest arsenal of firearms and set up the range, they smoked a huge brisket, and some friends agreed to bring over their horses. Some of Stephanie's friends even brought out their instruments and amps, which were quickly hooked up to the only power grid on the property.

While some rode horses, some hiked through the 200 acres of family land, and some sat aimlessly around a small fire and chatted, Stephen set up targets at the shooting range. There, an assortment of Stephanie's male friends inspected the various firearms and listened to gun safety rules. Most of the boys had never touched a firearm before.

A Town Called Sutherland Springs

After an extended lesson on gun safety and range rules, the shooting commenced, carefully overseen by Stephen. The boys' trash talked, and placed bets on who would be most successful. A few of the boys were decent shots. Not fantastic, but passable. Others let their trash talking get out of hand, only to fail miserably when they were called to prove themselves.

After a while, Stephen watched as Stephanie rode toward a strand of nearby trees, mounted atop the neighbor's large, dapple-grey horse. She reigned in the creature, and swung down from the saddle, handing the reins to one of her friends. Among the trees, a few idle horses grazed, awaiting their next riders.

Stephanie approached the range as a brief lull in shooting devolved into a smattering of more trash talk. She approached calmly, ignoring the bantering of her friends, loaded three magazines, each with seven rounds, and placed them on the old, worn-down picnic table which was peeling light blue paint in flaky curls. The table was a temporary fixture at the range. It served its purpose until money could be saved for new accommodations.

"Is the line safe?" Stephanie asked her dad.

He nodded.

Stepping through the weeds and tall grass of the field, she patiently set up twenty worn, tattered bowling pins, one by one, knocking them against the sand to be sure they were on solid ground. She walked back and fished a pair of earmuffs from the bag atop the table.

"Line's hot?!" She called out, as the teen boys slowly ceased their arguing, and watched curiously, taking steps back to give the girl space.

"The line is hot," Stephen replied.

Then, calmly, methodically, Stephanie began to shoot the bowling pins down, one by one. She moved down the line, dropping the magazine when it was empty, and reloading it with practiced hands. About ten pins in, Stephanie missed one, hitting the ground in front of the bowling pin and sending a small puff of sand flying into the air. She didn't hesitate, however. She simply moved to the next pin and continued down the line. When the last of the twenty pins fell over, hitting the sand with a thunking noise, Stephanie returned to the pin she had missed, aimed the gun, and fired her last round. The bowling pin fell back and hit the sand with a satisfied and triumphant thud.

The boys behind her stood in shock as Stephanie dropped her last magazine and placed it on the table, the slide of the gun locked open and facing upwards for the next shooter to see that it was empty. Stephen's heart swelled with pride as she smiled at him, pulled off the earmuffs, and turned, walking away from the range to rejoin her friends by the horses.

"Wait!" one of the boys called out. "You can't just do that and walk away!"

Stephanie shrugged at him and continued walking. "Yes, I can. I'm done."

Stephen smiled as the group of boys stared after Stephanie, their trash talk quieted, at least for the moment.

A Town Called Sutherland Springs

"Does she always shoot like that?" one of the boys asked, bewildered.

"Not really," he replied, as in the distance, Stephanie pulled herself back onto the dapple-grey horse. "She's a little off her game today."

The boy looked at him incredulously, as his smile widened.

"Normally, she doesn't miss."

✳ ✳ ✳

I was trying to get some sleep. On call was my least favorite time of the month: a time when I was never quite rested, and could never exactly make plans, because every time I tried, someone would break a toilet at the hospital, and I had to come running to get it fixed. A spraying sink, an overflowing toilet, hot sewage leaking down the halls of the hospital- any of these events would have my beeper going off, dragging me out of bed or away from the dinner table with my family. The next moment, I'd be pulling on my uniform to head into the hospital. Because of this, I spent a lot of my time on call resting and trying to catch a couple of hours of sleep before I had to rush off and deal with some minor, or sometimes major emergency at the hospital

So that morning, knowing that a week of rushing about was looming before me, I skipped church and stayed in bed. When I told my wife that I wanted to stay home, she didn't mind. Instead, she got up, dressed in worn out work clothes, and left the house to head out to our family land, to help my daughter and her husband build their tiny home. Alone in my room now, having nothing else to do, I drifted in and out of sleep, exhausted, and trying not to think about the week ahead.

It was while I was lying in bed that I heard a rhythmic tapping at my window.

Tap. Tap. Tap. I opened my eyes. Who would be tapping at my window?

Tap. Tap. Tap.

I blinked heavily, shifting in bed as the dull roar of the box fan in my room worked against the noise at my window, lulling me back to sleep, until my door burst open, banging against the wall. I looked up to see my eldest daughter, Stephanie. She stood there, hands dripping soapy water onto the faux wood floor of my bedroom, her bright blue eyes wide and full of mania. I sat up quickly, the look on her face driving action into my limbs without thought.

"What's wrong?" I barked.

"I think there is someone shooting at the Baptist Church," she responded breathlessly, her voice matching the mania in her eyes.

"It sounds like tapping at my window," I said jumping to my feet despite my skepticism.

"No, it's gunshots!"

Stephanie turned, leaving an unspoken urging for me to follow her as she fled from my room, her bare feet slapping down the hall as the tapping continued. I threw on a shirt as I rushed through my doorway, into the hall, and on into our kitchen. Here, it was louder. Here, where the insulation was older, the walls thinner, and the windows poorly sealed, I could hear each gunshot echoing through my house as if I was on a range. Each shot sent a cold pain like a knife through my gut.

My body sprang into action before my words could catch up. I was halfway down the hall to the laundry room before I called back to my daughter. "Call 911! And stay away from the windows!"

I didn't wait for her to respond. Instead, I rushed into the laundry room, pushing past a pile of laundry in front of my safe, and started working on the combination. As I worked, I opened my phone, and called my wife.

* * *

Kevin Jordan lay on his back on the asphalt driveway beneath his car, his hands covered in slick oil when the first shots split the silent Sunday morning.

At first, he was confused. The sound couldn't possibly be gunfire. He scooted out from under the car, curiosity driving him to his feet, as more shots rang through the silence.

As he stood, he looked in the direction of the noise. It was coming from across the street. It was coming from the Baptist Church.

There, he saw a figure clad in black, an AR-15 in his hands, spraying bullets at the front of the church and walking around the side, where the playground stood. Wood splintered and windows shattered.

Horror filled him, robbing his limbs of action as he watched what his mind could not process. He stood still for a moment, until the killer saw him.

Turning, the man fired three rounds in his direction. Kevin ducked and ran wildly toward his house in time to hear a bullet tear through his living room window, flying only a few feet from where his two-year-old son, Ezra, stood, his chubby little hands pressed against the glass, his long dark hair floating wildly about his face. Kevin burst in and snatched his son from the floor, kicking the door shut behind him and locking the bolt, only to run through the living room, grabbing his wife as he ran.

Gunfire continued as Kevin ran to his bathroom, hauling his wife and child with him. He tucked them into the bathtub and closed the bathroom door, bracing himself against it, as his family began to cry.

Fear transfixed him there, watching helplessly over his family as he desperately wished he had access to a gun.

✼ ✼ ✼

"Dad?" Kevin's panicked voice rang out on the Bluetooth speaker of Mike Jordan's blue Mustang.

Mike's wife, Lisa, glanced at him uneasily.

They were in La Vernia, on the way to H-E-B to get some grocery shopping done. They had just pulled out of the parking lot of O'Reilly's Auto Parts, and were headed through the center of town toward the grocery store.

"Kevin, what's wrong?" Mike barked out.

A Town Called Sutherland Springs

"Dad, get back here! Someone is shooting up the church!"

"What?! Are you kidding?" Mike asked roughly. For a moment, husband and wife looked at each other in disbelief. Surely, they hadn't heard him correctly. Surely, this wasn't happening. Not in their town.

"No, you gotta get back here! Someone is shooting up the church! Be sure you have your gun!" Kevin spoke too quickly- so quickly and panicked that his voice was barely recognizable.

Mike didn't hesitate this time. He slammed on his brakes in the middle of the highway and whipped the car around. Lisa's hands flew to the door to steady herself, her brown eyes wide behind slim glasses. As the car straightened out, Mike hit the gas and began flying down the highway back toward home, ignoring the cars around him and the 45-mph speed limit.

It was about a ten-minute drive back to Sutherland Springs. As the speedometer crawled toward a hundred, Mike knew he intended to cut the time down by at least half.

* * *

Lula Woicinski White was 71 years old. You wouldn't know it, though. Lula had the joyful spirit of a woman much younger in years. Her childlike sense of humor, and passion for life defined her. She lived every day to the fullest. Though Lula was plagued with numerous health problems, she refused to let them turn her into an invalid. Her favorite things were camping, dancing, and going to the beach. Lula and her daughter, Michelle, often went out to the beach at Port Aransas. They would bring low beach chairs and place them in the sand, where the waves would crash around them, and the sand erode beneath them. They would sit together, laughing as the waves barreled into them, the salty surf splashing up onto their bodies and sometimes into their faces. The first person who allowed herself to be bowled over by the water would lose.

In this game, Lula liked to cheat. If she felt herself falling first, she would often reach out and grab onto her daughter's chair, pulling her down into the water and sand with her. The game would end in hysterical laughter, and accusations. They both fell, she would argue, so Lula did not lose.

Even when it was cold, Lula still wanted to go to the beach. She could be found there, in the shallows of the ocean, bundled up in soaking wet sweats rolled up around her knees. She would be wearing a sweatshirt or a jacket, the hood cinched around a face beaming with joy, dancing in the freezing water, or collecting sand dollars and shells. It never mattered when her legs would get cold. After enough time spent in the water, they would go numb anyway.

Lula went out of her way to make people laugh. Whenever her son-in-law, Ben, came to pick her up for doctor's appointments, she could be seen leaving the house in the wildest outfit she could find. Oftentimes, this would consist of terribly mismatched shirt and pants, two different shoes, and two different socks visible beneath her shoes. She would leave the house beaming with pride, only to be turned around by Ben, who refused to take her into public dressed in such a manner. She liked to poke fun at her loved ones. She often went out of her way to pester them good naturedly and laugh at their exasperation. She was a stubborn, opinionated woman, whose faith was unshakable, and whose love for life was evident.

A year before the tragedy, Lula lost her husband, whom she had loved and stood by for 52 years. She was a faithful, loving wife who took care of her ailing husband and missed him dearly when he passed. Lula had been a member of First Baptist Church of Sutherland Springs for 18 years before she left this world to join her husband, and her Creator in Heaven, where there is dancing and hopefully, endless beaches.

✳ ✳ ✳

Julie dropped to the floor as the gunfire continued. The broken glass dug into the skin of her shins and her arms, but she didn't notice the pain.

"Someone call 911!" a voice called out.

She scrambled for her phone. As the screen lit up, she saw the time. 11:17. She dialed 911. The call failed.

Julie squeezed her eyes shut as the gunfire continued, each shot ripping through the walls of the chapel, tearing drywall, breaking glass, and shattering wood. Debris and dust choked the air as Julie prayed.

God. Stop this. Please stop this.

When she opened her eyes again, she picked up her phone. 11:18.

This time, the call connected.

"We are in the church in Sutherland Springs," Julie spoke quickly, her ears roaring, the gunfire spattering through the air. "Someone is shooting at us. Please send help! Please help us!"

The woman on the other line was quick in her response. "How many gunmen are there?"

"I don't know," Julie gasped. "Just help us! Please help us!"

At some point, Julie realized she was repeating herself. Over and over, asking for help. Just send help. Please help us.

"We are sending someone now," the woman responded.

Then, the operator hung up the phone.

Had she not hung up, Julie would have continued begging. She would have continued pleading for help. But, as the line went dead, so did the gunfire.

* * *

Hank Fahnert always knew he wanted to be a police officer. Since he was three years old, he knew one day he would make a living protecting his neighbors and upholding the law. La Vernia was his home. For a while, he worked in San Antonio. But as soon as he was given the opportunity to join the La Vernia Police department, he jumped at the chance. He had been with the department for eight years now.

Hank loved his job. He felt lucky every morning when he was able to put on a uniform and protect the community he loved.

A Town Called Sutherland Springs

So, when he got the call that there was an active shooter at the Sutherland Springs Baptist Church, Hank and his Sergeant sprang into action. They strapped on body armor, leapt into Hank's car, and sped toward Sutherland Springs as quickly as they could. On an average day, the journey from La Vernia to Sutherland Springs could take around ten minutes. But today, with their lights flashing, and their siren screaming, every car in front of them was going too slow, everyone they passed belligerently ignorant to their urgency.

* * *

Stephanie couldn't just stand there helplessly in her parents' bedroom, as the sound of each shot seemed to twist her organs tighter together. She couldn't believe there was actual gunfire. Not in this town. Not at the church. She had to see for herself. It was the only way she would believe. She barely listened as her dad barked a command at her and rushed to the backroom. Instead, she hurried to the front door, snatching her car keys as she ran.

Jumping into her car, she peeled out of the driveway.

She had to be wrong. There was no way this was gunfire.

There was a brief lull in the noise as she turned the corner of Fifth Street and drove up 539 toward the church. As she reached the corner of Old Highway 87, she saw why.

A shadowed figure stood paused for a moment before the front doors of the church. He was covered head to toe in black gear, and his face was concealed by a black, tactical mask. He held a rifle propped tight against his shoulder as he stepped forward, disappearing through the doors of the church.

Her breath caught in her throat as she made a sharp U-turn and rushed full speed back home.

Oh God, this can't be happening.

* * *

Julie dropped her phone and looked under the pews toward the giant double doors of the church. There, backlit by the sun, was a figure, clothed in black. In his hands, he gripped a rifle. His face was covered, and he wore black armor which covered his chest.

Julie did not hear him say anything. She did not see what he looked like. He was the faceless shape of evil, the dark form of Satan himself, and he was here, invading her church, her home. The congregants were silent, huddled under their pews as he stepped over the threshold, raising his gun, and opening fire once again. Julie looked for her sons. In the front pew, she saw the face of her eldest, Kris. He was huddled under the pew next to her. One row back, her youngest, Kyle, lay. Both were huddled up, as small as they could make themselves, staring down the aisle where the murderer methodically approached.

"Is the back door unlocked?" someone whispered through the gunfire.

"No, it's bolted," her son, Kyle, responded.

If anyone were to try and unbolt it, surely, they would become the main target for fire. That way was barred, leaving the only avenue of escape the double doors blocked by the murderer clad in armor.

Julie squeezed her eyes shut again. Her hands gripped the ground tightly, nails digging into the thin carpet. She heard his soft footsteps approaching. When he walked by, she would grab his feet. She would grab them as soon as she could. She would pull them out from under him. He would fall, smash his head on the ground. He would be knocked unconscious. She could grapple for his gun. She could stop him.

No, she couldn't. If she was strong enough in her fear, to pull his legs out from under him, and if he fell, he may not be knocked unconscious. With all the adrenaline and evil intent running through him, the chances of him being knocked unconscious were slim. And, if he fell, he would then be face to face with her son, with a gun in his hands. She would have just facilitated the death of her own son. No sooner had she thought this, she opened her eyes.

She opened her eyes to the barrel of a gun, pointed directly at Kris's spine. The crack of the bullet was followed by a puff of gun smoke. Kris cried out in pain. Julie reached out to him and gripped his hand.

"Shut up," she silenced him.

Kris did not make another noise. With her words, though, the murderer turned to her. The rifle fired, and Julie's arms wrapped around her body as a bullet buried itself in her chest.

* * *

In 2006, Julie was diagnosed with breast cancer. This came as a complete shock to her. No one in her family had ever had cancer. There was zero history of it. There was no reason for her to have cancer. Throughout her battle, Julie received chemotherapy. In the end, she had to undergo a double mastectomy.

For a long time, she struggled with this battle. She didn't understand why this was happening to her. She didn't understand why this illness came out of nowhere. She hadn't been prepared for this. Why had God let this happen?

She found herself in a state of bewilderment when she learned she had to have her breasts removed. This wasn't fair. It didn't make sense.

In the end, Julie clung to her faith. She knew God had her best interest at heart, even if she didn't understand His reasons. So, she tried to trust in God's plan as she went through reconstruction surgery.

Because they had removed her entire breast, the doctors had to pull muscles from her back around to rebuild her chest. They added an implant and stretched the muscles around it.

Julie didn't understand at the time that all this trauma, all this pain, and all these surgeries, had been preparing her for a much bigger day. A day in which Julie would be needed more than she would understand.

Because, after the murderer shot her in the chest, he moved on.

Maybe the monster had assumed the new dress she was wearing was covered in blood from bullets, instead of large red flowers, or maybe he assumed the single bullet wound to her chest had been enough to kill her. Little did he know, God had prepared Julie for this day.

The bullet would have been enough to kill someone else. But not Julie. Countless reconstruction surgeries had replaced muscle, where most only had tissue. Because of her breast cancer, because of her double mastectomy, Julie's reconstructed breast stopped the bullet from penetrating her body further. God used breast cancer to save Julie's life.

Chapter Three: A Call to Arms

Pam scraped the thick, white plaster off the drywall tool, into the dirty red bucket. She was tired already. All morning, she had been at the house her daughter and son-in-law were building. The small home was a much bigger project than they originally thought. When the idea first occurred to them, the entire family got caught up in the optimism of the plan. They knew it would be a big project to build their own house. There were many things they needed to learn, things like how to hang insulation, drywall, and how to run wire and copper pipe. To their surprise, however, it wasn't the big things like that which posed the most challenge to them. It was the smaller details which were taking much longer than anticipated: things like floating and taping, fixing strangely built corners, and going back and building false walls to correct mistakes.

Pam, her daughter Rachel, and son-in-law Matt had spent almost every weekend for the better part of the last year and a half working out here, in blazing heat or brisk cold, trying to fulfill a dream which had seemed so much easier a year and a half ago.

They were almost finished now. The plumbing and electrical work were finished, the insulation hung, the drywall in place. The only remaining details were those small, pesky finishing ones, like floating, taping, and mudding the walls.

Pam was a perfectionist, but not in fact a mudder. Since this was her first time, her work was never good enough for her taste, and ever since she had discovered her daughter was pregnant, the pressure was on to have the house finished.

She had just sent Rachel and Matt back home. Rachel was suffering from morning sickness today, and Pam had refused to let her help mud the walls.

"I'm not going to be here long anyway," Pam had told her daughter, who was pale and exhausted. "I just have to clean up these tools, and then I am coming home, I promise."

They had been reluctant to leave. Pam had a way of doing too much and exhausting herself. She was a stubborn woman. So was Rachel. In the end, Matt had to force his wife into the car.

"Don't stay too long, ok?" Matt told her. "Otherwise, I won't be able to keep Rachel from coming back out here."

"I'll be home soon," Pam promised.

Shortly after they pulled away and headed back toward Sutherland Springs, as Pam was washing the grey mud from the bright red bucket with hose water that was so cold it made her hands ache, her phone rang. Putting aside the hose and wiping her hands dry on her paint-stained and torn green work pants, Pam picked up her phone. It was her husband, Stephen. She answered.

"Hello?"

"Pam, where are you?"

His voice was quick and clipped. It took a moment for Pam to recognize the panic in his tone. Her heart quickened, as a sense of dread began to creep up her throat.

"At Rachel's house, I'm wrapping up now-"

"Stay there," he interrupted. "There is an active shooter at the Baptist Church."

"What?" she responded, disbelief and confusion making her voice tremble.

Active shooter? There couldn't be. Not here. Not in Sutherland Springs. This couldn't be real.

"Stay there," he said again.

Fear clawed at her as she realized what was happening, as she realized what her husband would do next.

"Stephen," she croaked. "Don't you go up there!"

It didn't matter. Before she could finish the sentence, he disconnected the call. As the line went dead, Pam let out a cry, lifted her eyes to the gray sky, and began to pray.

✷ ✷ ✷

When I was a child, I spent a lot of time with my great-grandfather, Big Daddy. Big Daddy was a staple in the community, a man known for his loud laughter, kindness, and steadfast faith.

True to his moniker, Big Daddy was a large man, who had a deep raspy voice, and loved to tell stories. Stories about the depression, and how, when his family had finally received their stamp to buy a car, he had taken it into town and traded it for a flatbed truck. It didn't even have a closed cab. Momo

A Town Called Sutherland Springs

was furious when he came home. She had been looking forward to styling around town in her very own car. But Big Daddy had plans. He used that truck to haul supplies into the small town of Sutherland Springs throughout the depression, providing the people with what they needed to make it through the tough years. My great-grandmother eventually forgave him for getting that ugly old pick-up, although it took quite a bit of time, and convincing.

One of the clearest memories I have of my great-grandfather was the old man's hands curling around me, lifting me up, and letting me ring the bell in the steeple of the First Baptist Church of Sutherland Springs on Sundays, to call the worshipers to service. I still remember the way the rope felt rough in my small hands, the way the loud clang of the bell echoed throughout the small town, the people streaming in through the double doors of the chapel, and my great-grandfather's smiling eyes.

* * *

It wasn't a bell ringing now. It was gunshots — gunshots so loud each one was like a stab in my chest. As I hung up the phone, cutting my wife off mid-sentence, I heard the front door slam open and flurried footsteps rush down the hall. My daughter burst into the laundry room as I reached into my safe, her eyes wide with shock and horror.

"Dad, there's a man in black tactical gear shooting up the church!" she cried.

I looked at my daughter for only a moment. She was already weeping.

Tactical gear. I turned back to the safe, grabbed my AR-15, and a handful of bullets from an unopened box of ammunition. Pushing past her, I rushed into the living room, cramming the bullets into the magazine. Stephanie followed at my heels.

"Stay here," I told her as I tore open the door.

"Dad…" she started, following me onto the porch, tears choking her voice.

I knew she would follow me if I let her. She would follow me anywhere. That couldn't happen.

"Load me another magazine and stay here!" I commanded, not even pausing to put on shoes.

✳ ✳ ✳

When I was twelve years old, I went on a long-haul trip across the state of Texas with my father. My father was a truck driver and was sometimes gone for weeks at a time. Sometimes, during the summer months, when I wasn't in school, Dad would take me on his trips. I cherished this time with him, when it was just the two of us. When there was no one else to get in the way. No one else to share the attention.

It was a long haul across Texas which brought the two of us to the small, obscure diner in the middle of a town whose name the world forgot. There wasn't much that was special about it: it could have been any diner, in any small town across Texas which was a popular stop for truckers, transients, and locals. It was, however, special to me, as was any time spent with my father.

A Town Called Sutherland Springs

It was late. Probably in the middle of the night. A trucker's schedule was a fluid thing — he stopped when there was a place to stop. He slept when he was tired. As long as he made the delivery on time, the rest didn't much matter.

There were only two other tables in the little diner which were occupied. One was a man and a woman, talking quietly over lukewarm coffee, and pancakes with syrup forming sticky puddles on the plate. The other was a man. Broad shouldered and gruff, the man watched the couple from the corner of the diner.

My Dad and I didn't take much notice of him until he strode over to the couple, grabbed a handful of the woman's hair, and smashed her face into the table.

Dad was on his feet in an instant. I was right on his heels as he rushed over to the table to pull the giant man off the woman as he threw her to the ground.

The man at the table was faster. He pulled a gun and aimed it at the attacker before he could do anything else. We pulled up short as a waitress squeaked in fear from behind the counter.

"You there," the man with the gun said, glancing quickly over at me. "There are two police officers outside. Go get them, please."

I looked at my father for only a moment before turning and running for the door.

When I returned with the two officers in tow, my eyes searched for my father. He stood between the woman and her attacker, apart from the man with the gun. I joined him.

Time passed. Eventually the man with the gun approached us and introduced himself as an off-duty police officer.

"I appreciate how quickly you reacted," he told my dad. "It is good to know that if I wasn't here, someone would have done something."

"It's our job as men," Dad replied. "We are the protectors."

The officer looked at me. I was standing there, in my father's shadow.

"How old are you, son?"

"Twelve."

The officer smiled. "What do you suppose you would have done?"

"Helped in any way I could, sir," I replied sheepishly, understanding how young I was, understanding I might not have done much more than get in the way. "I was following my father's lead."

The officer chuckled slightly. "Raising him right, I see," he said, nodding at my dad approvingly.

"Men shouldn't be still when someone needs help," Dad responded. "Stephen knows that."

* * *

Rachel was on her way back to Sutherland Springs. Her husband, Matt, drove; their two dogs clattering in the backseat, buzzing with energy, covered in sand and grass burs from their brief jaunt at the family property.

A Town Called Sutherland Springs

She was sick today. Only a few months pregnant, she was deep in the throes of morning sickness. It had put a tension on a Sunday that was supposed to be packed full of family plans: a birthday party, dinner with the in-laws, and another chance to see her precious niece and nephew. But today was strange. Today felt ominous. From the moment she woke, she knew that something was wrong with this day. The anxiety and gnawing fear were squatting in her chest, compressing her lungs and stomach, making it hard to breathe.

As they drove down the road toward Sutherland Springs in still silence, Rachel's phone rang loudly, picking up on the car's Bluetooth. It was her mom, Pam, whom she had just left behind at the construction site of their home. Matt and Rachel made brief eye contact.

"Great, what did we forget?" he asked with a slight chuckle in his voice.

Rachel shrugged and answered the phone.

"Hey, mom..."

"What's going on?" Pam demanded, panic straining her voice.

Matt glanced over, confused.

"Huh?"

"What is going on?!" she repeated, louder, more urgent this time.

Rachel's heart quickened at the sound of fear in her mom's voice. Her mom wasn't afraid of anything.

"N-nothing," she stuttered in response, trying to remember if she had done anything wrong.

"Where are you?!"

"On our way home," Matt responded, bewildered.

Ahead, they saw the stop sign in front of Rachel's parents' house, their current place of residence until they could finish construction on their own home.

"Turn around and get your ass back here now!"

At the sound of her panic Matt didn't even hesitate. He slammed on the breaks and pulled a quick U-turn, speeding off in the direction they had come.

"Pam, what is going on?!" he asked as he straightened the car, the dogs clapping together in the back seat and grunting in protest.

"Mom, you're scaring me," Rachel added, feeling suddenly very much like a child.

"Well, I'm scared too," Pam answered. "There is a man shooting up the Baptist Church, and your dad went up there with his gun."

✳ ✳ ✳

Rachel was nervous. All her life really, had been training her for this moment. Gun safety had been drilled into her brain since she was old enough to understand words.

Stay away from those, they are dangerous if you don't know what you are doing.

These are powerful tools. You must treat them with respect.

A Town Called Sutherland Springs

If you ever see one of these when you are alone, do not touch it. Walk away and get an adult immediately.

Rachel had spent hours sitting on the carpeted floor of the living room, watching her daddy disassemble the firearms, scattering intricate pieces - springs, triggers, pistol grips, scopes, and barrels - all over the floor in fixed patterns. Stephen inspected each piece carefully, cleaning them with old ripped up t-shirts dipped in a strong-smelling dark liquid.

The scent of gun cleaner was just as synonymous with her childhood as cheerios and grandma's chocolate cake.

Still, Rachel was nervous. It was her turn to hold a gun, to aim it down the tightly packed dirt of the range at the large white and black targets. It was time to use the knowledge she had been given. She was nervous, not only because she had been taught the raw power which these tools held, but also because she wanted to do well. She wanted to be able to prove she could handle them.

Rachel's friends stood behind her. They were watching. None of them were nervous anymore. They had already taken their turn.

When it was time to shoot, Heather, who was a year older than Rachel, had bounced forward eagerly, while Rachel had hung back. Heather was nine, after all. She knew what she was doing. Confidently, she had pulled her long, blonde hair back and tied it with a scrunchie, donning her safety glasses and approaching the range table with practiced respect. Heather's father had handed her the magazine, which she loaded with confident hands. When Rachel had loaded her magazine, her little hands shook slightly and fumbled, pulling down the spring as she tried to cram in the .22 bullets. She even dropped a few on the sandy concrete.

The only thing that kept her calm was the presence of her father. He was a quiet strength behind her. He saw her hands shake when she loaded the magazine and picked up the scattered bullets before she could. He helped her pull down the spring as she loaded the bullets one by one into the magazine. He put his large, calloused hand on her shoulder. His comforting wink produced an uneasy smile from her.

"You don't have to do this if you don't want to," he said.

He mistook her nerves for fear. She wasn't afraid, per se. She just knew the power of the tool in her hand and wanted to do well. She shook her head.

"I can do this," she responded.

Her father smiled reassuringly as she pulled on the old, slightly scratched safety glasses and approached the range table. Sitting in the beat-up metal chair, Rachel put her hands flat on the table as her dad stepped up beside her. He put the .22 Browning in front of her.

"Is it loaded?" he asked.

This is when Rachel's hands moved. She had practiced this before. She took the gun carefully, pushed the button to drop the magazine, and placed it on the table. This one was empty. It took effort to pull back the slide and lock it. Her hands were small, but she knew what she was doing. As it locked into place, showing an empty barrel, Rachel felt proud.

"Good," her dad said. "Don't ever, ever forget to do that every time you handle a firearm. Even if you just saw someone check to see if it was loaded, you have to check again. Understand?"

She nodded.

"Remember how to load it?"

She nodded again, picking up the magazine she had prepared, and slamming it into the pistol. It took two hands to pull the button to release the slide. It sprung into place with a loud click. Rachel flipped the safety on and carefully laid the firearm down on the table, with the barrel pointing downrange, as she had always been taught.

Don't ever let this barrel point toward anything you don't want destroyed, her dad had told her, over and over. It makes no difference if it was unloaded. Rachel had been taught to treat every firearm as if it was locked, loaded, and ready to fire.

"What do you do now?" her dad asked.

Rachel looked up. "Is the line hot?" she responded in almost a whisper.

"They can't hear you, baby," he answered with a widening smile.

"Is the line hot?" She repeated louder, this time looking to her left and then to her right.

The adults there took a step back, with broad smiles and nodded.

"Line's hot!" her Uncle Mark announced from the left.

"The line's hot!" Heather's father, Terrell, responded from the right.

Stephen Willeford & Rachel Howe

Rachel looked up at her dad before she did anything else. He nodded, his bearded smile reassuring. She could do this. With him here, she could do anything. She pulled on her earmuffs- these giant, clunky things, which always seemed to squeeze her head. Stephen sat down in the chair next to her as she picked up the pistol, propping it up on the sandbags. She wasn't quite strong enough to hold it up safely yet. Stephen helped her with her hold, adjusting her hands on the grip of the pistol. He talked her through lining up the sites and pointed downrange at the black and white targets stapled to the splintered wooden backing. Behind that, a berm made of reddish sand loomed, prepared to stop stray bullets. Green weeds and sunflowers grew from the top and sides of the berm, swaying in the slight summer breeze which swept across the range. Rachel's friends, and the adults around her were respectfully quiet as she clicked off the safety on the pistol. The button now showed red. Red means' hot. Red, for fire.

Rachel centered the sights, and aimed at the target closest to her, taking a deep shaky breath.

"Take as much time as you need. And remember, when you're ready, squeeze the trigger. Don't pull it."

Rachel took a while to breathe and steadied her nerves. She took time to get used to the feel of the metal in her hands, and the way the crisscross pattern of the grip felt on her palms. After what seemed like an eternity in the oppressively hot Texas sun, she was ready.

Carefully, she squeezed the trigger, keeping her eyes focused on the sights and the target. The pistol fired, a loud clap of noise. Though she had heard it many times before, it seemed too loud, regardless of the earmuffs. Rachel was surprised at the kick of the firearm. It bucked in her hands as if trying to escape. Her grip held, however, and she did not drop the pistol. Instead, she slid her finger off the trigger, and looked up at her dad, smiling at him with a swelling sense of pride. She had done it. She had fired. Her dad was smiling back at her, the same pride reflected in his gaze. She looked back downrange.

"Did I hit it?"

"You did. Look! Near the seven."

There, amid the black ring of the seven, was a small bullet hole. It wasn't in the inner circles, but at least it was on the target. Rachel beamed with pride.

"Want to shoot the rest of the magazine?"

She nodded, picking the pistol back up and aiming. As she took the next few shots, missing or barely grazing the target each time, she began to feel discouraged.

After about five shots, her dad motioned for her to stop. She laid the pistol on the table again and slipped the earmuffs off one of her ears. Was he going to tell her to stop because she wasn't good enough?

"You're anticipating each shot," he said. "You're tensing up, and jerking the trigger, because you're scared of the recoil. You have to relax. That's why you aren't hitting the target anymore. It isn't because you can't, it's because you're getting too eager. Take deep breaths. Slow down. There is time for speed when you're older."

She nodded and pulled the earmuffs back on. For the next four shots, she took her time. She breathed deeply between each squeeze of the trigger. She was still slightly afraid of the recoil, but she tried to relax through it. When the magazine was empty, the slide locked back, she laid the pistol back down on the table and pulled off her earmuffs.

Her dad smiled down at her. "Let's go look at your target. What do you do now?"

She dropped the empty magazine out of the pistol. Once that was done, she put the pistol on the table again, chamber up and muzzle down range.

"Is the line safe?" Rachel asked loudly.

"The line is safe!" Uncle Mark and Terrell responded.

She stood, and together she and her dad walked around the table and headed downrange. Even though she did not hit the target all ten times, and even though she didn't hit anywhere near the center x, she could hear the pride in her dad's voice as they pulled the target from the staples. She had hit it four times, across the seven and six circles, one bullet even hitting the very edge of the eight ring.

"You did great, baby doll," her dad was telling her. "And you'll only get better from here as you get used to that recoil."

Rachel knew she hadn't done fantastically. Heather had hit the target nearly every time. She had even hit the nine and ten ring a few times. But it didn't matter. Her dad was so proud she may as well have hit the center. You would have thought she had.

Sundays were passed in this manner. Stephen's oldest daughter Stephanie, Rachel, Heather, and a handful of other kids their age would go to Blackhawk Range. While their

A Town Called Sutherland Springs

mothers practiced on the range next to theirs, training for the women's league, the men trained the kids. They practiced loading and unloading the pistols and checking the chamber to be sure it wasn't loaded. With unloaded guns, they practiced squeezing the triggers. They talked about gun safety and taught the kids how to be comfortable holding the gun, while still having a healthy respect for it. Practice made perfect. Every Sunday, they shot at targets, working on levels of expertise set out by the NRA. Each week, they got better and better. When the mothers were finished with their practice, the dads would trade ranges with them and the kids would go play in the woods far behind the range.

Stephen, Terrell, Mark, and Lance would practice with their pistols and rifles, over and over again. They competed against each other even in practice. They did drills together to sharpen their skills and their reflexes. It was all a hobby, though. All for enjoyment. Stephen never thought these drills would ever be put to use outside of those Sunday afternoons at the shooting range. He never thought the skills he practiced repeatedly, would one day save lives. Stephen always said he hoped to be the kind of man who would defend someone in a terrible situation. He hoped he would have that kind of courage, but never expected to need it.

He had spent years training, running drills to narrow down accuracy. Competing against his friends, and even in the occasional tournament. He had even built a range on the family land, where he liked to take people and show them his collection of firearms.

The second amendment was important to him. Gun ownership ran in his blood. He had always defended this freedom with every fiber of his being. Never did he think he would need to use it. Little did he know, all those hours logged at the range and the gun show, all the rounds he had shot, the hours of target practice, gun safety training, and dinners spent discussing his hobby were God preparing him for a day in his future.

✷ ✷ ✷

I leapt off our concrete porch, into the long grass, my AR-15 tucked tightly in the crook of my elbow as I scrambled to load the fistful of ammunition into the magazine. I could hear the loud gunshots still ringing out. It was a foreign and terrifying sound in my once peaceful little town.

I crammed the magazine into the gun and pulled back the bolt. The satisfying click of the firearm loading barely registered as I sprinted across the front lawn, into the street.

My heart jumped with every crack of a bullet, winding my nerves ever tenser, making my legs pump faster than I had run in years. Each bullet fired was another stab, another reminder of how painstakingly long it took to wrest my gun from the safe, run outside, and load my firearm. Each gunshot was a reminder that I wasn't there yet, and I couldn't get there quick enough.

I barely felt the ground beneath me as I ran across Highway 539, my bare feet slapping hard on the hot asphalt. My mind didn't register the heat. It was as if I didn't even touch the ground.

As soon as my feet hit the highway, and I could see the church in front of me, my vocal cords tensed on their own, my mouth opened, and I shouted, my voice ringing out above the gunshots, gruff and enraged. I didn't know what I said, or even why I spoke at all. With my shout I had given up any tactical advantage I may have had, any element of surprise. But my voice was not my own, it was taken over by someone greater than me, a need greater than my own safety to call out the evil inside the church.

At the time, I didn't know what I said. But it didn't matter. Because my daughter, crying out to God in the living room of our house heard me. The people huddled and praying beneath the pews in the church heard me. And as my voice rang out, and the gunfire ceased, I knew that evil had heard me also.

* * *

It was Saint Patrick's Day, 1984, when Debbie met Keith. She had just started working at Chelsea's Street Club in San Antonio. He was in Basic Training for the Army. Clad in a green skirt, peasant blouse, and fishnet stockings, she waited on a handsome man, dressed in a United States Army uniform. The electricity between the two was immediate. Debbie talked him into drinking a green beer. He asked if she could join him after her shift.

Company policy kept Debbie from doing so, and disappointed, she went home, convinced she would never see Keith again.

Keith, however, was determined. That night, after dinner and drinks at the pub, he went out and bought Debbie a stuffed rabbit and a card. He already knew he loved her.

He returned to Chelsea's and left the rabbit with another waitress, to give to Debbie when she returned. Over the next few days, Keith found rides from friends on post to the pub, showing up night after night to see her, hoping to catch one of her shifts.

It took a few days, but eventually Keith saw Debbie again. When she saw him, she was surprised and delighted, both by his persistence and the soft, cuddly rabbit he had left for her. They talked for hours. She gave him her phone number and left that night, again, never really expecting to hear from him.

But Keith kept calling her. He even met her daughter and took them both to the zoo. They spent as much time together as possible over the next few weeks before Keith was reassigned to Georgia, where he would attend the United States Army Airborne School, known as "Jump School". When he left, Debbie was once again plagued with doubt. She was sure this time she wouldn't hear from him anymore.

But as soon as Keith settled in at post, the very first thing he did was call Debbie. Actually, every night while he was in Georgia, he called her. Though the long-distance charges continued to build up, Debbie and Keith both knew it was worth the money. This was real love. When Keith received his orders to move to Germany, Debbie took a bus to Georgia, leaving her little three-year-old daughter, Becky, with her mother. After she arrived, they caught a flight to Pennsylvania where they met Keith's family. They went to the courthouse. They were married by a Justice of the Peace that afternoon, on May 31st, 1984.

A Town Called Sutherland Springs

Debbie and Becky followed Keith to Germany a few months later. When they arrived at the airport, Keith picked them up in a borrowed car, brought them to their small apartment, and cooked dinner. Well, he tried to cook dinner. The spaghetti he made was little more than corkscrew pasta, and unseasoned tomato paste. It was terrible, but remains a fond memory of Debbie's. It didn't really matter that it was terrible because he was trying so hard.

Keith didn't just love Debbie; he also loved her daughter as if she were his own. Once, during a trip to the zoo in Germany, Becky dropped her favorite toy. It was a stuffed Gizmo, from Gremlins which had just come out in theaters. Chubby, overeager baby hands had let it slip while leaning over the animal enclosure. Gizmo fell, landing on a ledge inside the lion's den. Becky began to cry, convinced her toy was gone forever. Keith would not let that happen. Not paying any mind to the dangerous cats lounging in the sun, he bent over into the animal pen, reaching as far as he could and scooped up Gizmo. From that moment on, Keith was Becky's hero. A few years later, the first chance he had, Keith officially adopted Becky as his own.

That is the way Keith always was. His wife and three children were the most important things in the world to him. No matter what happened, Keith worked hard to be sure his family was loved and cared for. When Debbie had a bad day, he brought her flowers, or another stuffed animal. There is a shelf in Debbie's house now, filled with stuffed bears and rabbits, whose warm eyes and soft fur remain a testament to Keith's overwhelming love. Among them is Thumper, the small and now worn, stuffed rabbit Keith bought the day they met.

Keith hid notes for Debbie before he left for work in the mornings, slipped under her pillow or placed on the counter. He often drew silly faces on them or reminded her how much he loved her. When their granddaughter, Zoe, caught on to this, she demanded notes as well. This began a playful back and forth. Keith would write a note to Zoe, and Zoe would draw a picture of them together and leave it for Keith. They shared a special bond and spent many hours reading together or just being goofy. Keith adored his grandchildren.

All three of Keith and Debbie's children were baptized at First Baptist Church in Sutherland Springs. Debbie was as well. It was their home, the place where they all renewed their faith and dedicated themselves to God. Keith and Debbie were married for 33 wonderful years before Keith joined his Creator in the house of worship they so loved. Debbie's greatest comfort is knowing that one day when the time is right, they will have another dance in Heaven.

Keith Allen Braden had been a member of First Baptist Church of Sutherland Springs for 25 years.

Chapter Four: Exchanging Fire

The pain from the gunshot wasn't what Julie expected. She had expected to be immobilized. She wasn't. She could still breathe. She didn't think she was dying. She couldn't believe she was alive after being shot in the chest, but she was. Suddenly, she heard the gun go off, rapidly, and panicked against the far wall. She looked over in the direction of the shots and saw too many still figures.

Twenty-eight shots, one right after the other, tore through the air, until he had emptied his magazine. Why had he emptied his magazine into people whom he had already killed? Julie turned away from Kris and looked for Kyle.

Kyle was gone. The pew under which he was hiding was empty.

The murderer turned back to Kris, drawing his pistol, and fired another round into Kris' side. The noise of the gunshot impacted Julie's heart, causing all breath to leave her body. Her son didn't make a sound.

The panic in Julie's chest blossomed into a frenzy as she watched the murderer exit the church, his pistol drawn, the rifle no longer in his hands.

As he exited, she turned toward Kris.

"Kris, are you ok?" she gasped, reaching her hands out to him. Her hands were covered in blood and broken glass.

Ok? How could he be ok?

"I'm fine," he responded, his face ashen from fear and blood loss. "But mom, I can't feel my legs."

* * *

The old western town rose around Blake, a marvelous, strange thing. His family was here on vacation. Blake, a young boy of only seven, sat on the wooden bleachers in the dusty streets, surrounded by old saloons and banks. People dressed in western clothes, with revolvers strapped to their waists, led horses through the town and called out to the tourists. Blake sat beside his dad, Stephen, a broad, hulking man who was immensely pleased to be there. His mom was on the other side of his father and his two older sisters were talking with her.

They were in Tombstone, the old southern town turned theme park. The show was starting soon. The Earp brothers, and Doc Holliday would face off against the band of ruffians who had nicknamed themselves the Cowboys. The performers were beginning to gather as the crowd settled down on the bleachers behind a thick, red velvet rope.

Blake was buzzing with energy, barely able to sit still on the bleachers. His mom and dad had told him all about the shootout at the OK Corral when they were on their way here. He couldn't wait to see a real-life western sheriff showdown against a band of ruthless outlaws and ruffians. But they were there early, as they always were. Blake's dad didn't believe in being on time. If they weren't at least fifteen minutes early, they were late.

Blake watched anxiously as a tall man approached the red velvet ropes, wearing a large cowboy hat and a bandana around his neck. The star emblazoned on his chest marked him as the Marshall.

"Look, Blake, that must be Wyatt Earp," said his mom, pointing at the performer.

Blake bounced in excitement, reaching out and touching the soft rope with little, fluttering hands. The Marshall whistled loudly, silencing the tourists who had arrived early hoping to get good seats. None had gotten seats as good as Blake and his family though. Of course, none of them had arrived nearly thirty minutes early.

The chattering died down. Tourists raised cameras and fanned themselves with pamphlets and hats. The Arizona heat was inescapable, even in November.

"Before the show starts, while we wait for everyone to arrive, we have a little demonstration for you," Wyatt announced, his voice thick with an exaggerated southern drawl. "We'll need a volunteer. Who wants to help us out?"

Stephen whistled and pointed down at his son. Blake gripped the red velvet rope hopefully.

Wyatt's partner nudged him and pointed to the eager child.

Wyatt smiled. "How about the littlest in the crowd? How about it, son? Want to come help us?"

Blake couldn't believe it. They were talking to him. He looked up at his parents nervously.

"Go on, son," his dad whispered to him excitedly.

One of the performers stepped forward and lifted the red rope, beckoning to him. His dad watched as Blake ducked under it and approached the performers.

"What's your name, son?"

"Blake."

As he approached, one of the men placed a red bandana on the dirt behind him, setting two Ruger Vaquero revolvers on top.

"Where are you from, Blake?"

"Sutherland Springs, Texas," he responded.

"Ah! A Texas boy, huh? Well, Blake, we have a little demonstration we need help with, but you'll need to use your imagination, ok?"

Blake nodded.

"Now," Wyatt announced. "Imagine you are playing on the playground in Texas. You are running around with your friends, and you climb up a slide!"

Blake smiled. Wyatt approached him and placed a hand on his shoulder, spinning him around to face the revolvers and crouching down to his level.

"As you slide down it, you see these two guns on the ground in front of you! Can you tell which one is real? One of them is fake."

Blake looked down at the firearms and shook his head. "They both look real to me," he said without hesitation.

"They do, don't they? But are you sure? Want to go over there and check?"

Blake shook his head decisively. "No, sir. I'm not supposed to touch guns."

Wyatt looked surprised. He glanced up at his fellow performer for a moment, a smile forming on his lips. "Well then, son, what're you going to do?"

"I'm going to tell my mom there is a gun in the playground, and she will take care of it so we can keep playing," he responded, in a very matter-of-fact way.

Wyatt straightened, his smile widening. "That's right, Blake!" he responded. "Now, these guns are real for our show, but the bullets are what are called blanks." He tapped the gun at his waist. "Is it ok to point them at someone and fire, since the bullets are only blanks?"

Blake looked up at the man in wide-eyed shock. "No, sir! You never point a gun at another person, even if it's unloaded. My dad says to treat every gun as if it's already loaded."

Wyatt looked down at the little boy with admiration. "Sounds like they are teaching you right, down there in Texas," he responded. "Who are your parents, boy?"

Blake pointed toward the crowd of tourists. It was easy to see which parents were his. His father beamed from the bleachers, his bearded face glowing with pride.

"Blake is absolutely right," Wyatt announced. "Even though these bullets are only blanks, they still have the potential to do great harm. Watch this!"

Another performer stepped forward as Wyatt led Blake back toward the stands. He placed a Dr Pepper can on the fence, drew his gun, and fired at point blank range. The crack of the bullet pierced the air and the can popped open, spraying soda everywhere.

"The point is, these firearms are tools, but they are dangerous ones," Wyatt announced. "Put in improper hands, and treated without respect, they could really cause a lot of damage. Everyone, please give Blake here a round of applause for knowing the answer to every question!"

The audience applauded loudly, but none so loudly as Blake's dad.

"Next, I want to give a shout out to Blake's parents for teaching him right! Of course, we should expect nothing less from such fine folks from the great state of Texas! Give them a round of applause as well!"

The audience applauded again.

The bleachers were now full, ready for the performance. Wyatt clapped Blake on the back and thanked him once again for his help, raising the ropes for him to slip under as he announced the beginning of the show. The boy rejoined his father, and the show began.

It wasn't a long performance. After all, the real-life showdown at the OK Corral only lasted about five minutes. The show was marvelous anyway. The tourists cheered as banter was exchanged, guns were drawn, and shots were fired. Blake gasped as Wyatt's brothers fell to the ground, wounded. Wyatt and Doc were not to be cowed, however. They prevailed, taking out all the Cowboys and dragging the brothers to safety. The audience applauded as the show came to a spectacular end, and the performers bowed and thanked the crowd for coming.

As tourists gathered their kids, shouldered their cameras and backpacks, and slowly milled away to visit the other attractions of Tombstone, Wyatt approached Blake and handed him the Dr Pepper can. It was signed by the entire cast.

"Here, kid, a souvenir," Wyatt told him with a broad smile.

"Thanks!" said Blake, taking the slightly sticky can from him and searching through the crowd to find his sisters. He absolutely had to rub it in their faces.

The performers lingered behind. "You're his parents?" Wyatt confirmed, shaking Stephen's hand heartily.

"Yes, we are," Stephen responded, the pride unmistakable in his voice as Wyatt turned to his wife, Pam, and shook her hand as well.

"I want you folks to know, we've been doing this a long time to teach gun safety. We always grab a kid from the crowd. And your kid is the first to get all the answers right. You both are doing a great job."

"I'm an NRA certified instructor," Stephen responded. "We have a youth shooting team in Texas. I've been training that boy in gun safety since he was born."

"So he was the perfect one for you to pick," Pam spoke up proudly.

Stephen Willeford & Rachel Howe

"Yes ma'am, I guess he was! Few folks teach their kids about gun safety so young. It's good to see someone doing it correctly."

"Well, as you heard, we're from Texas. We like our guns in my town, so you've got to teach the kids right."

✶ ✶ ✶

As I ran into my neighbor's yard, my AR-15 clutched tightly in my hands, my feet pounded through the grass over sharp sticker burrs, and teeming anthills, the pain of which did not penetrate the determination that filled my mind. Every beat of my heart sent adrenaline coursing through me, adrenaline that sharpened my senses. With every breath came an iron resolve that bolstered each bound of my legs and prevented me from shaking.

Time slowed as I rushed forward, as if the world had suddenly been paused. In the middle of the street in front of the church, a gray Ford Explorer idled. The soft hum of the engine trickled through the air, and the driver's door hung open and ready. The car faced the highway for a quick escape. Then I saw the church, the once pristine white chapel now faded from years of love and service. Its doors hung open, dark and empty like a mouth open in a terrible scream. The walls, windows, and doors were riddled with bullet holes, the wood splintered, the colorful blue and purple glass shattered. The quiet coming from inside the church was more deafening and frightening than any noise I had ever heard.

From those terribly silent open doors, he emerged. Concealed in a black tactical helmet, strapped in black body armor, the killer exited the church. He looked left and right, searching for me. He carried himself upright and stiff, exuding confidence. He raised his hand, which gripped a pistol, and pointed it at me as I ran toward him. His movements were jerky, as if he was nothing more than a wooden puppet, a marionette on invisible strings.

I heard the loud crack of gunshots echoing through the air as he pulled the trigger. I could see the pistol kick in his hands and the movement of the slide ejecting the casing and chambering the next round before he fired again. I saw the brass fall to the ground, the sunlight shimmering off it for only a moment before it disappeared into the grass. As I sprinted into the driveway of the Curnow's yard, I heard the bullet crunch into the truck in front of me, tearing through metal. More bullets whistled past me as I ran between Fred's Dodge pickup truck and Kathleen's bright red Challenger. A bullet buried itself in the wooden siding of their house as I rushed past.

Slapping my rifle across the hood of the pick-up, I aimed, bringing the EOTech Red Dot Sight up to my eyes. I centered it on the killer's armor-clad chest. As I aimed, I remembered my training, and remembered a conversation with a friend many years before.

"Even if they are wearing armor, shoot them center mass," I could hear Lance say. "They will feel it."

Lance was formerly Army Airborne. Now a police officer, he trained San Antonio police SWAT teams, police snipers, and occasionally my shooting team. We jokingly called ourselves the Sinners. In archery, you sin when you miss the target. We were a group of men that gathered on

Sundays after church to fellowship, shoot, and compete against other teams.

Lance was one of us. He attended our church, his wife was friends with mine, and his kids were friends with my kids. He was a tall man with a deep voice and a gruff personality. Regardless of his rougher edges, the man was our friend and definitely knew how to handle himself around a firearm. One day, for no particular reason, we all stood around talking to him about how to take down an active shooter.

"Body armor may protect him, but if you put a bullet in it, it will definitely get his attention," he told us. "That shot will feel like a sucker punch."

With Lance's voice echoing in my ears, I peered through my sight, my hands practiced and steady. I fired twice without hesitation, once for the killer's chest, once for his abdomen. As the rifle fired, I watched the killer pause as one by one my shots hit their mark. In that moment, his demeanor completely changed. His air of false bravado drained away, and it seemed that the strings controlling him were suddenly cut. I recognized the exact second that his fight turned into flight. Gripping his pistol tightly in his hand, he began to run for his vehicle.

No. He was not getting away. Not now. Not after what he did. This man rained hell on my community- he was a wolf attacking a flock of innocents.

Well, if he was a wolf, I was a sheepdog. And I was trained by my Shepherd for this day, long, long ago.

As the killer ran around his car, I heard Lance again.

A Town Called Sutherland Springs

"After you get their attention, look for an opportunity: there are three weak points to aim for. Aim for the leg, the hip, and the side. Those are the most vulnerable spots. The legs will slow him down. The hips will stop him. The side will kill him."

We were in the hot Texas sun, at Blackhawk Shooting Range southwest of San Antonio. The reddish dirt covered our boots as we heard shots all around from the surrounding ranges. Standing around Lance in a small circle, my friends and I watched as he pointed to his leg, his hip, and his ribs.

"The way body armor straps to you exposes your sides with just Velcro," Lance explained, pointing at his rib cage. "That will be the most vulnerable point on the armor to hit him. Also, if you can hit him in the leg, or hip, it will really slow him down. Just make sure your bullets count for something."

Make them count for something.

As the killer turned to jump into his Explorer, he lowered his guard for a split second and exposed his side.

I lined up my rifle and squeezed the trigger. I watched the bullet penetrate his side and saw him stumble again as I aimed a second time. As the second bullet impacted his leg, the killer fell into his vehicle, hauling the door shut behind him. He raised his pistol again, crossing his right arm across his body with the gun nearly pressed against the glass of the driver's side window. He fired twice. Although I knew I could hear the shots, my brain barely registered the noise as I watched each bullet open a hole in the Explorer's window. Delicate cracks like spider webs spread out from where the bullets punched through the glass. I watched- as if in slow motion- the small shards of glass from the hole fall toward the ground and tinkle as they bounced against the asphalt.

I didn't duck. I didn't hide below the truck, out of sight. An unearthly and surreal calm had taken hold of me. God was taking care of whatever came toward me as I peered through my rifle again. Glass crunched as one of the bullets buried itself in the windshield of the Challenger behind me. Wood splintered as another hit the siding of my neighbor's house. I could only pray that the Curnows weren't home and were somewhere safe.

As for myself: I knew that I didn't need to worry about the bullets coming in my direction. I felt the hand of God on me, protecting me, curling around me in His power and deflecting the killer's aim. I knew I would be safe and knew I had been sent here to complete a task. I prayed that my aim would be true.

The killer began to pull away, the bright Texas sun glaring in his window, obstructing my view of him. I aimed my rifle again at the driver's side window, toward the bright prism of sunlight. Lining up my sight with where I perceived his head to be, I squeezed the trigger again. The window collapsed, sending glass scattering across the road and into the lap of the driver. His tires squealed as he pulled away, turning onto 539 and slamming on the gas. The Explorer swerved and accelerated, rushing down the highway. This wasn't over. There was another church, just miles down the road in the direction he was heading. I couldn't let him leave and start again somewhere else.

A Town Called Sutherland Springs

I ran out from behind the pickup, sprinting out into the middle of the highway. I raised my rifle again, steadying my breathing and zeroing in on the back of the killer's retreating vehicle. The familiar rifle rested firmly against my shoulder, gripped lightly and comfortably in my hands. I had built this rifle. I had chosen every feature myself and customized it for accuracy in a firefight. Before this day, it had all been theoretical and a mere hobby. Now, I knew that it was God that had designed my rifle for this particular day. And I trusted He wouldn't fail me now.

I breathed in as the killer's car accelerated down the main street of my town, passing by my neighbors and friends: skidding past the roads where my wife and I had been on walks with our children, and the playground at the church where they used to play. I let the oxygen fortify my nerves and calm the adrenaline, fear, and disbelief that was coursing through me. I lined up my sights on the rear window of the Explorer as it approached without hesitation the only blinking red light in our town, about 150 yards from where I stood. I centered the red dot in the back of the driver's seat and squeezed the trigger one last time.

As the crack of my rifle split the air, the back window shattered, scattering glass in haphazard shards across 539. The killer floored it again, his retreating car jumping over highway 87 without even pausing. He crested the hill at breakneck speeds before disappearing from my sight. It couldn't end like this. So help me God, he wasn't going to get away.

Ignoring the hot pavement, I lowered my rifle and looked around wildly. The morning was now terribly silent as I turned, searching for a way to pursue. That is when I saw a large pick-up truck idling at a stop sign across the highway from the church, a young man with wide, stunned eyes behind the wheel. Carrying my rifle on my shoulder, I began to run across the highway toward him, swinging my arm and shouting desperately.

✳ ✳ ✳

Jennifer Massey- whom most people called Jenni- moved in with the Holcombe family in 2007, when her parents moved from Wilson County to Kingsville. She could have gone with her parents, but she felt drawn to this area. She knew God was calling her to live among these people, and her story here had just begun. Initially, she didn't see Karla and Bryan's son, Marc Daniel- who everyone referred to as Danny- as a romantic interest. She liked him well enough but wasn't really looking to date. Oftentimes, however, when she was home at the Holcombe house, Danny would get back before everyone else and they would talk for hours. It did not take very long for them to become best friends.

"You don't think there is anything between them, do you?" Karla once asked her daughter Sarah, while peeking around the corner at Danny and Jenni. The two were on the couch, laughing and talking. There was electricity between them: a perfect chemistry which was easy, laid back, and completely natural.

"I don't know," Sarah had responded. "But that would be so great!"

Everyone close to Jenni and Danny knew what was going to happen before they themselves knew. Their friendship was so comfortable and intimate that it begged a greater purpose. Although they didn't know how or when it happened, friendship deepened into love. They never went on regular dates; they just spent time together going on long walks through the woods on the family land, laughing at Danny's strange jokes and planning world domination. Danny was kindhearted, eccentric, and had an odd sense of humor which Jenni really enjoyed. Jenni laughed easily, and Danny had been enamored with her since the beginning.

Less than a year after moving in with the Holcombes, Danny and Jenni got married. The news surprised no one. It was easy to see they were made for each other.

Danny loved being a husband. He told everyone, even strangers, about his wife. He was so proud of her that for a long time she was practically all he could talk about.

Danny was a mechanic at F&W Electrical in Floresville. There, he was known as the company's MacGyver. Danny was very gifted with his hands, dedicated, and extremely inventive. When the company, or anyone for that matter, needed something fixed, he would be their first call. He could create things out of nothing, and fix things which most people had already abandoned. So thoroughly did he fix things that they had a slogan: "The Holcombe Overkill." When Danny fixed something, it would last a thousand years.

Danny loved everyone and had a special ability for making everyone feel incredibly important. The reason for this was simple: to Danny, all people were incredibly important. He would do anything in his power and go completely out of his way to be sure they knew. Everyone he knew always received a hug from him. He was always this way. In fact, when he was young, on his way to school, he always had to stop and give the crossing guard a hug. Always. Danny was never one who could walk by the same person every day without bringing a little joy into their life. Everything he did was for other people.

Though Danny was an amazing husband, his true calling was that of a father. Originally, Danny and Jenni struggled to conceive. Their journey to parenthood was a long and difficult one. After years of trying, fertility treatment, and thousands of earnest prayers, Jenni finally became pregnant. Both of them were elated. Danny, however, could hardly contain his excitement.

Before Jenni was pregnant, back when their child was a fervent prayer to God, Jenni was spending her daily time in scripture. She was reading Numbers 27. Here, scripture recounted the tale of a man named Zelophehad, who died after having five daughters and no sons. The daughters, knowing they would be left destitute without a brother, pleaded with Moses to beseech God on their behalf. When Moses brought this matter before God, he was told the women could keep the inheritance from their father, in the absence of a male relative. One of those daughters was named Noah. The name struck Jenni. She was inspired by the woman's ability to stand up for herself and her sisters, and to plead with God for help. Jenni knew that if she ever had a daughter, she would want her to be named Noah in honor of this woman.

When Jenni and Danny found out they were having a girl, they were ecstatic. Immediately, Jenni remembered Noah from Numbers. Danny wasn't convinced at first. They went back and forth, finding other names and changing their minds, only to constantly circle back to Noah. It was the meaning which finally sealed the deal. Noah meant motion, and from the moment of her first kick, their child was in constant motion. Whether it was the hiccups or twirling in the womb, the small child could never seem to be still.

On May 17, 2016, Noah Grace Holcombe was born. When she was born, Noah had inhaled amniotic fluid, and Jenni was able to hold her for only a moment, and snap a quick picture, before they rushed her precious daughter away to NICU. Danny followed. For twelve hours, Jenni was unable to visit her daughter- her greatest comfort was in knowing that Danny was by her daughter's side as a strong and faithful guardian. From the moment Noah arrived, she and Danny formed an unbreakable bond. Everyone always joked that Jenni was all Danny would talk about, but it all changed when Noah came. He lived for her. If anyone even mentioned in passing that she was cute, Danny would stop them in their tracks to show them pictures and videos of his girl.

One particular video was his favorite. Once Noah was mobile enough to crawl throughout the house, she discovered she could get a drink out of the water dispenser. Whenever she was thirsty, she would toddle over to the dispenser, stand up, and suck a drink out of the faucet like a hamster.

"Look how smart she is!" Danny would beam as the random stranger at the supermarket, gas station, or on the sidewalk watched with a polite smile.

No one could escape news of Danny's girl. Not that anyone wanted to. Noah was the cutest and sweetest baby. Her joy lit up a room, and her constant, never-ending motion kept her mother incredibly busy. The child rarely slept. Now,

Jenni knows it was because Noah had so much to do, so much to see in the short time she blessed the world. She couldn't waste time sleeping. Jenni quickly grew accustomed to the fact that sleep was a temporary thing. It wouldn't be long before little hands stirred, patting her anxiously, ready to play, or until she heard Noah's little voice babbling in the next room, anxious for a snack or to see her beloved mama's face. Jenni would patiently get up and hold her daughter close to her, pulling out toys and playing while Danny slept.

Although Noah had the beauty of her mother, she acted just like her father. She exuded his joy, made the same faces, and was persistently happy. Never had Sutherland Springs seen a child so young with such an overflow of personality. Before she could form words, Noah was already talking. She would point to things she wanted and babble. She would pick things up and converse with them, in a child's language.

Once, when Noah was playing with her cousin Elene in her grandparents' shop, and Elene walked away, Noah burst out in a scolding stream of nonsense. Although she was not using any discernible language, it was evident she was chewing Elene out for leaving her behind. Noah's iron will and personality only strengthened as she grew. She was a very opinionated child who would let you know exactly what she wanted, whose vocabulary belied her age. Noah loved lollipops, vegetables, her cousins, and animals very much. When the two family dogs followed her around the house, licking her, rubbing against her, and flopping dramatically into her lap, Noah would squeal with delight and bury her chubby little hands into their fur.

A Town Called Sutherland Springs

When Noah was old enough to walk, Jenni would often find her daughter standing in the kitchen in the middle of the night, illuminated only by the moon and the blue light of the microwave. Noah's tiny hands would grip the handle of the refrigerator tightly and pull with all her might, her little bare feet squeaking against the kitchen floor.

"Don't want!" she would call out. "Don't want!"

Jenni was never sure why she would say "don't want," but it always meant the same thing: Noah wanted Jell-O.

The memory of late nights curled on the kitchen floor with a spoon and a cup of Jell-O, laughing and cuddling little Noah, is a great comfort to Jenni now.

Jenni and Danny had been married for nine and a half years when they went to church on November 5th, 2017. Danny and his 18-month-old daughter went to join the Author of their lives that day, where they will always be together and lovingly, patiently await Jenni's arrival.

Although the pain of their absence is strong, Jenni now lives to honor them both. She knows they are together and watching over her every day.

Danny Holcombe was a member of First Baptist Church of Sutherland Springs for three years, and little Noah Grace had been attending since she was knitted together in her mother's womb.

* * *

Johnnie Langendorff was idling at a stop sign in Sutherland Springs. He could hardly believe what he was seeing; a small town transformed into a war zone. Across the street, a man with a gun, in tactical gear was clambering into a car and firing his pistol at another man, who was standing behind a black truck, his gun across the hood, firing back.

The man slammed his door and began to streak away, turning wildly onto the highway and gunning his engine. His back window shattered as he disappeared down the road.

What the hell?!

Johnnie looked back over at the church as the other man – a short, stocky man with no shoes and wild eyes – came sprinting toward his truck, a tan AR-15 gripped so tightly in his hands that his knuckles were white.

It seemed surreal as the man approached his passenger door at full speed.

"That man just shot up the Baptist Church," the man cried, rage in his voice. "We have to stop him!"

Johnnie didn't hesitate. He unlocked the door.

"Get in!" he called, a split-second decision causing him to stomp on the gas pedal after the shoeless maniac clambered into the car. Slamming the door shut, they sped off down 539, crossing Hwy 87 without even slowing down at the stop sign.

* * *

As Hank and his sergeant barreled toward Sutherland Springs, the drive seemed to take longer than he thought possible. Their sirens whirled, the police radio squawked loudly, and conflicting reports poured in as they swerved through traffic, drawing ever closer.

There are multiple shooters.

A Town Called Sutherland Springs

The shooter had left the scene.

The shooter was still there.

They weren't sure about the status.

Hank glanced at his Sergeant, who rode grimly next to him. They were going in blind. They had no idea what they were walking into.

Regardless, Hank wasn't afraid as they raced closer to the church. He was trained for this. He had been prepared to protect his neighbors since he was a child, playing cops and robbers with his friends. Hours spent in seminars and participating in active shooter drills had prepared his mind and body for this day.

He was born for this job.

If only he could get there faster.

Chapter Five: Triage

"Lisa, do you have your pistol?" Mike asked his wife as Sutherland Springs loomed before them.

Wordlessly, Lisa reached into her purse, pulled out her pistol, and handed it to her husband. Mike turned the Mustang into the town, the familiar houses blurring past as he flew down Business 87. Ahead, he saw his neighbor and lifelong friend, Stephen, jump into an idling Dodge with an AR-15 gripped tightly in his hands. The truck sped off and disappeared as Mike approached.

Mike pulled into his sister-in-law's yard and leapt from the car, gun in hand. He crossed the street to the church quickly, eyes alert, looking for the monster with the gun.

Kevin rushed from his house, running across the street to join his dad.

"He's gone," he said breathlessly. "Stephen went after him."

Mike lowered the pistol, and he and Kevin turned towards the doors of the church which hung open and foreboding.

* * *

A Town Called Sutherland Springs

Julie didn't move until she heard tires squeal. As soon as they peeled away, she got to her feet, picking up her phone again.

Julie was a nurse. For thirty years she had worked in emergency rooms, and operating rooms. The nurse in her began to take over as she opened her phone. 11:28. How had it only been ten minutes? Julie felt as though she had been hiding under the pew for a lifetime.

The operator picked up the phone.

"The gunman is gone," Julie told them. "Please send EMS. There are people hurt."

She barely listened to their response. Instead, she hung up the phone, and the nurse inside her took over.

Somewhere in the church, Gunney, a war Veteran, began to speak.

"Praise God," he said as loudly as he could. "Praise God. Even now, praise God."

Gunney repeated himself over and over as she began to move through the chapel, checking her friends and neighbors for injuries. She needed to triage. When the EMS got there, they needed to know who to help first. She moved through the church, checking her loved ones for signs of life. She checked for a pulse by the pulpit and found none. Sorrow rose, building and building as she moved on from those she could not help, and continued to search through the pews for survivors.

It wasn't until she saw the little girl in the Cinderella dress that all her calm, all her surgical experience vanished. It was then that Julie began screaming.

Stephen Willeford & Rachel Howe

✷ ✷ ✷

Dennis and Sara Johnson were married for 44 years. Their relationship was defined by their unshakeable faith and deep love for one another. It wasn't always this way, though. When Sara and Dennis met, Sara worked at a bar called the Hot Spot, and Dennis was an alcoholic. He had been heavily drinking since he was 14, but, after the sudden death of his first wife, he had taken up the hobby as a lifestyle. Sara had two children: Jimmy, and Deanna. Jimmy was the same age as Dennis' son, Neal. The two were best friends and would often play together in the bar parking lot while Sara waited tables and Dennis drank.

Soon after, they were placed together at a party with their friends. Dennis was not a dancer, but Sara forced him to join her on the dance floor anyway. She would soon regret it when she saw his dancing skills. That night, Dennis drank so much that Sara wouldn't let him drive home. She drove him back to her place instead and let him sleep on the couch.

After that, Dennis spent a lot of time with Sara, intent on dating her. Although she resisted at first, soon enough, he persuaded her to join him on a date, and their relationship blossomed. They were married July 27, 1973, and blended their families of small children together.

After a while, however, Sara grew weary of Dennis' habit. Although he was a hard worker, and always made sure to pay the bills on time, Dennis spent a good part of his waking hours drunk. Finally, Sara had had enough. One night, she gathered their four children- Neal, Jimmy, Deanna, and their newborn baby boy Michael- in the living room. She packed up Dennis' belongings in worn suitcases and waited for Dennis to get home from the bar. When he arrived, tired and smelling like liquor, Sara gave him an ultimatum: his family, or his liquor. He broke down and made the right choice. He chose his family, but knew he couldn't do this alone, and begged Sara for help. This began the deepening of their relationship. After this conversation, they turned to God.

It was during a church service, at the final song, when Sara closed her eyes and prayed, as the congregation sang around her. She prayed for the strength to walk up to the altar and accept Christ. She knew she needed him desperately in her life, she knew he was calling her to leave the pew, but she was afraid to go by herself. She prayed earnestly for the strength to go, for the push to walk up the aisle and submit her life to Christ. As soon as she opened her eyes, Sara saw Dennis stand and leave the pew. It turned out, just as God was working on Sara's heart, he was also working on Dennis'. Sara watched for a moment in surprise, as her husband stood and made his way to the front to pray with an elder. Then she quickly stood and followed at his heels, his commitment and bravery providing her with the strength she needed.

Christ redeemed both Dennis and Sara. This redemption started them on a journey to share the gospel with everyone they met. No one was too far from God, too sinful, or too lost for Dennis and Sara to love. Their home was always open to anyone in need. They were actively involved in the prison ministry, and any form of outreach. Dennis was a deacon in the church, led Bible studies, and mentored young men. Sara helped with the food ministry, volunteered in the kitchen, and helped teach Sunday school for the children.

Dennis was defined by his steadfast faith. He was deeply dependable. Whenever anyone needed anything, he would be the first to ask, and if there was a problem, Dennis could fix it. His experiences and struggles made him wise and insightful. He had a way of making everyone around him feel safe and secure. He worked hard to provide for his family and community and was very straightforward and honest. Every word he spoke was a lesson his children and friends took to heart.

Just as Dennis was serious, Sara was sarcastic. She was a spitfire and had a quick, scathing wit and jocular personality. She was playful and teased everyone she loved. She was a strong, opinionated woman, with a deep love for people, and an even deeper love for God.

They were the nucleus of their family. Everyone gathered at the Johnson house for holidays and reunions, knowing that their house was a safe haven from judgment. They never turned anyone away.

Through their testimony and strength, Dennis and Sara brought countless people to Christ. Dennis, 43 years sober, stood as a powerful example of God's redemption. Dennis and Sara believed God could reach anyone, and lived their lives reaching out to the lost, broken, and hurting.

Dennis and Sara died in each other's arms on November 5th, 2017, in the church they loved, worshiping the Father who had saved them both, and entered Heaven's gates hand in hand. They had been members of First Baptist Church of Sutherland Springs for eleven years.

* * *

"Julie!" Gunney bellowed, attempting to struggle to his feet. "This day did not take God by surprise!"

His voice was powerful, forceful. It silenced Julie's animalistic scream. He was wounded, bleeding, yet he stood tall. He looked at her with confident eyes, and spoke again in a loud, clear voice.

"You have been prepared for this day. Do what God has trained you to do!"

His words pulled Julie from her screams, from the dark place of horror in which she had descended. There would be a time for mourning, but she didn't have time now. There would be time to cry for the children lost, but that time was not now. With tears in her eyes, she turned away from the little girl.

"Gunney, sit down," she commanded. "You're shot."

* * *

Later, when this horror was all over, when the survivors gathered to mourn and recount their terrible tales, Julie would thank Gunney for his words. They pulled her from the fear and terror that had frozen her. Gunney, however, did not remember saying anything to her. Later, Julie and Gunney would realize God had spoken directly to her and said exactly what needed to be said so Julie could work to save the other injured congregants.

"If God can speak through a donkey," Gunney would say, "Surely he can speak through me too."

* * *

Gunney slunk to the ground.

"Ms. Julie," a familiar voice spoke. "If you don't come help me, I am going to bleed to death."

Julie turned toward the voice and saw 18-year-old Zachary Poston. He was pale, and bleeding profusely. Bullet holes riddled his arms, legs, and torso. There were seven in total.

The nurse in Julie started to take over again. Tourniquet. She needed a tourniquet. Julie ran from the church building. As she turned to bolt across the lawn, she noticed thirteen discarded magazines lying empty in the grass. Thirteen. She had stepped over more in the sanctuary.

She ran to the children's Sunday school classroom. Sometimes she left rags in there. She always had a few extra tucked away in corners of the church. People always used to mock her for it. She collected rags from the OR and stashed them in different places. She was never sure why. Maybe it had been for this day. She burst through the door to the classroom, the brightly colored toys and posters out of place and distorted by the fear and adrenaline coursing through her.

Julie began tearing through drawers and cabinets, pushing aside supplies, books, and crayons.

* * *

Peggy Lynn Warden was a loving, tender person. She cared deeply for the people in her church, especially the children. Not only did Peggy help with the food pantry, but she also cleaned the kitchen at the church, taught children's Sunday school, and helped lead Vacation Bible School every year. Peggy was a creative, crafty person. One year, when the church needed a Statue of Liberty for its VBS display, Peggy created one using an old t-shirt, Duct Tape, and a tomato cage. She always did things like that- whether it was an impromptu Statue of Liberty, Tie-Dye shirts, or a submarine- if there was crafting to be done, you could bet Peggy was at the head of the group.

Peggy loved to garden. She spent many long days pulling weeds and watering fruits and vegetables. Then, when they were ripe, she would pick them, can them, turn them into jam, or bring fresh bags of produce to her family and to church. The red cherry tomatoes were so sweet they could be eaten like candy.

Peggy lived to serve others. She was exactly what she seemed- a genuine Sunday school teacher who never had a harsh word to say and always had an encouraging Bible verse to help you through your day. She treated everyone as if they were her own flesh and blood. Peggy was everyone's mother, and never met someone to whom she was not motherly, and sweet. There was not a single mean bone in Peggy's body- she just didn't have it in her to make anyone feel less than special.

She extended the same affection to animals as well. Whether it was an injured calf, or an abandoned neighborhood dog, Peggy constantly brought home strays. For a while, her family was even convinced that she had a secret pet skunk that could be found slinking around the property and scratching at the door for food. The smell didn't matter to her. There really was no creature Peggy couldn't love.

Stephen Willeford & Rachel Howe

In the 39 years that Peggy was married to her husband, Christopher Warden, she was the traditional housewife. Dinner was ready on the table at 6:00 every evening and the house was spotless. The two of them loved each other deeply and cared for each other until the end.

Christopher was diagnosed with lung cancer in June of 2016. Shortly afterward, Peggy was diagnosed with early-stage breast cancer. When she was admitted to the hospital for surgery, Christopher slept in his car in the hospital parking lot so he could be close to her. Though his cancer had progressed to a point where he was weak, and struggled to walk, he would walk up to her room to visit her every time she was awake. He cut up her food when she was too weak to do so herself. When Peggy was released, Christopher was admitted into hospice. She cared for him until he passed away in July 2017.

When the shooting started, Peggy passed away in the same way that she had lived: in the service of others. As the shots rang out, Peggy turned her back to the murderer and wrapped her arms around her grandson, Zachary, taking a bullet which would have likely killed him. No one who heard of her sacrifice was at all surprised. Peggy protected and cared for everyone- no matter the consequences. She had been a member of First Baptist Church of Sutherland Springs for 23 years. Her family's greatest comfort lay in the knowledge that she had joined a husband she dearly missed, and a Heavenly Father to whom she had dedicated her life.

※ ※ ※

A Town Called Sutherland Springs

Rusty Duncan was on his way to pick up a grill. A church up the road on FM 775 was having a yard sale. They were selling a very nice propane grill, and some lawn chairs. It was exactly the kind Rusty had been looking for. He had stopped by earlier that morning and paid for it- only to realize he couldn't load all of it up by himself. So, he had traveled back home to pick up his truck, and his sixteen-year-old son Jase.

He got the call as he was driving down 87, through the tiny town of Sutherland Springs.

"There is an active shooter situation in Sutherland Springs," the fire chief's voice spoke over his phone's speaker. "Stay out of there, we don't know anything yet. Stand by for more information."

Rusty was already in Sutherland Springs, about to pass by the post office. Active shooter? He slowed his car down and pulled into the parking lot.

Rusty and his son did not speak as they looked around the small town. Cars drove past, rushing down 87. The gas stations were there, open, and seemingly quiet. He heard no gunshots. Maybe it was something small. Besides, it was just a normal Sunday. Nothing appeared out of the ordinary. He circled the post office parking lot, pulling out onto FM 539, and facing the heart of town, idling for a moment at the blinking red light and watching for anything out of the ordinary.

It had to be something small. A lover's spat. A disagreement over property lines. A stray animal wandering too close to someone's chickens. There was no way it was something big. Not in this town. Not on such a quiet Sunday morning. Rusty waited in his truck, his son at his side, a growing sense of dread creeping into the atmosphere.

* * *

"No," Pam snapped on the phone, gathering her things together. "Stephanie, listen to me, you stay inside. You go into your room, and you stay away from the windows!"

Pam was washing her hands in the cold water from the hose. There was mud and plaster all over them. Panic beat at her chest as she prayed fervently for the safety of her husband and her town.

This couldn't be real.

Stephanie was panicking. Her voice was reaching hysteria on the other end of the line. All Pam could make out was that she wanted to leave the house. She wanted to know where her father was.

Of course she did. But she had to be safe.

"No, Stephanie," Pam replied, as a yellow Kia pulled into the driveway. "Stay home! I am coming home now. Don't you dare leave that house!"

Matt and Rachel spilled out of their car, fear and concern evident on their faces.

"Ok," Stephanie finally conceded, her voice thick with tears. "Ok, but please hurry."

Pam hung up the phone and switched off the hose.

Rachel stepped forward. "Mom, what is going on?"

Pam wiped the water off her hands onto her shorts. "I don't know. Your dad went up there with his gun."

"He went up there?" Matt responded.

Of course, he did. The shock was evident on Rachel's face. Her knees shook as she tried to understand what she had just been told.

Dear God, keep my Daddy safe.

She thought of her unborn child, a child whose presence everyone in her family eagerly awaited. For a terrifying moment, she wondered if her baby would ever get to meet her grandfather.

"Where are you going?" Rachel asked as Pam strode toward her car, keys in hand.

"Home. Stephanie is panicking and wanting to leave the house. I have to be there with her, and I have to know what's going on."

"Is it safe?!" Matt asked incredulously, his hand landing on his wife's shoulder.

The concern for the safety of his wife and child was clear in his voice.

"Stephanie said the shooting stopped," Pam answered, getting into her car. "I think it's over. I am going now."

"We're coming too," Rachel responded, rushing back to their car.

The door wasn't even shut before Pam turned the keys in the ignition and began pulling out of the driveway. Her heart was in her throat, the blood roaring in her ears louder and louder the closer she got to home, as the sound of sirens screeched through the air.

✶ ✶ ✶

Sarah pulled into the familiar parking lot to the church, the gravel crunching beneath her tires the only noise which broke the stillness of the morning. The clock read 11:30. She waited for a moment, debating if she should just go to the nursery. She could go there first, and get Elene set up. Surely, the lesson had already started. Her dad was preaching today. She could sneak into the back after dropping off her daughter.

In the midst of these thoughts, there was a loud rap on her window. Startled, Sarah looked up to see a neighbor standing there, his eyes wide and glazed with a frenzied look of shocked panic. He was pale. For a moment, Sarah thought she should just pull away.

"You've got to get out of here," the neighbor, Kevin Jordan, was saying. "There has been a shooting. You can't go inside; you have to get out of here."

A shooting? Fear pierced her as she put the car in reverse, more out of a reaction to Kevin's panic than his words. The words were foreign to her. They almost seemed to float in the air in front of her, meaningless, descriptive words which had no place in this small town, on a Sunday morning that should have been just like any other. A shooting...

Sarah pulled away from the church. She had to get Elene to safety. Whether the safety was from the danger that lurked in the church, or the hideous, foreign danger of that inexplicable sentence from the neighbor, Sarah wasn't sure. She just knew she had to get out of there.

She swung around the block and pulled onto the next street. There, she saw another neighbor: Lisa Jordan, Kevin's stepmother. Lisa stood helplessly in her yard, looking small and lost. Sarah pulled over and rolled down her window.

"Lisa, what's going on?" she asked, her heartbeat getting louder and louder in her ears.

"There was a shooter at the church," Lisa responded, brown eyes wide and brimmed with tears. "I think a lot of people didn't make it."

Sarah struggled hard to grasp her words. The morning looked so quiet. So ordinary. There was no way this was true. Not here. Not in Sutherland Springs. Not at her church.

Her whole family was in that church.

The shock that filled Sarah drowned out all noise. All noise but the incessant roaring of her heartbeat. It filled her every sense, seeming to suck all color and sound out of the day as Sarah rolled up the window, hands gripping the steering wheel so hard her knuckles were white. Her heartbeat, assaulting her senses like the harsh slam of a jackhammer drowned out the nearby sirens. Ambulance lights whirled by, unseen by Sarah as she tried to process that hideous, horrifying sentence.

Sarah picked up her phone. She had to get a hold of her parents, her brothers, anyone.

With shaking fingers, she began to dial.

* * *

Stephen Willeford & Rachel Howe

In high school, Karla Plain was very shy. One of seven children, Karla wasn't quite sure how to speak up for herself and struggled with confidence issues. Naturally, when she met a boy in school who was outgoing, friendly, and funny, she was drawn to him. Everyone who knew Bryan liked him. He wasn't exactly one of the "popular" kids, but he was eminently likable and always knew how to make people laugh. He treated everyone as if they were his close friends. Karla quickly developed a huge crush on him, although she wasn't exactly sure if he knew she existed. She was much too shy to approach him, so she was certain her crush would remain silent and unrequited.

However, on Valentine's Day, when Karla was fourteen, the Student Council did a fundraiser. They sold carnations to be delivered to your crush. Carnations happened to be Karla's favorite flower. The simple beauty in the delicate layers of petals, the varying colors, and the way they looked like the twirling petticoats of a dress made this flower gorgeous. It didn't even occur to Karla that she might receive one.

So, when she attended her first class and found a beautiful carnation with her name on it, she was delighted. Although her name was on the flower, the sender was anonymous. Surely, this flower had come from one of her siblings. She was quiet, shy, and existed mostly unnoticed by the general population of her high school in Victoria, Texas. Surely, this flower must have just come from a member of her family.

She repeated this story to herself multiple times, so her hopes would not get too high. Secretly, though, her mind was already racing. Could it be from him? Had he truly noticed her?

As the day progressed, Karla received another mystery carnation. Her excitement grew into elation. Who was this mystery admirer?

She wouldn't have to wait long to find out.

In the hall, between classes, she spotted Bryan with a carnation in hand as he approached her through the throng of high school students. Her heart beat wildly in disbelief as he handed her the flower. It turned out that while she had been watching him in admiration, he had been doing the same.

This was the beginning of a loving, and playful relationship which spanned nearly half a century. In 1977, right out of high school, Karla Plain became Karla Holcombe. Together, with her husband Bryan, they had four children: John, Danny, Sarah, and Scott. Their relationship was defined by a playful teasing. The married couple loved to poke fun at each other and laughed constantly. Through Bryan and her faith in Christ, Karla became a more outspoken and confident woman.

Everyone who knew her, knew about her faith in God. The Holy Spirit shone through the actions of her daily life. Karla saw His hands in everything. A sunset could bring her to thankful tears.

"He painted that sunset for me," she would tell her children, gazing at the splash of colors brushed through the evening sky. "God, thank you for creating such a beautiful sunset for us!"

Stephen Willeford & Rachel Howe

Karla always knew how to make any situation fun. With just a look, she could make her friends devolve into laughter. She was joyful and silly, and used her hilarious personality to make people smile. Once, when one of her children left their lunch at home, she showed up at school dressed as a clown- crazy wig and giant spotted pants included. Suffice to say, it was a long time before her kids forgot something again.

Karla lived to serve others and went above and beyond to make every experience amazing. Family affairs were always a party. Karla would plan huge events for everyone, such as Easter egg hunts for kids and adults alike. For adults, the hunt would involve riddles, challenges, and dares. Inside the eggs, money, candy, or small trinkets would be hidden. Some were so well hidden that her family is sure there are still Easter eggs scattered around on the family land, serving as little plastic reminders of Karla's intense love for her family.

Karla lived for her grandchildren. Her house was the one where messes could be made, beds jumped on, and walls climbed. The kids would spin until they were dizzy, run through the house like barbarians, and be as loud as they wanted. Snacks of sugar, candy and soda were always provided by a grandma who would let her grandkids have anything they wanted. Mini meringue cookies were the traditional snack.

"Grandma's house, Grandma's rules," she would say, her eyes sparkling with joy as her grandkids played elbow deep in baked goods.

Meanwhile, her loving and devoted husband laughed along with her. His grandkids called him Grumpy after an inside joke ran rampant. Like a giant person being named Tiny, Bryan Holcombe was anything but Grumpy. He was the kind of person everyone wanted to be friends with. He was outgoing, fun, and eccentric. Laughter came easily, and he was a natural storyteller. Once he started talking, he would go into all sorts of extraneous details, following many rabbit trails so that one story morphed into twenty before he was finished. His daughter, Sarah, would poke fun at him, labeling his stories with numbers so she could keep track. She would remind her dad when he began to repeat himself. It didn't matter to him, though. He could retell a story a thousand times, with the same excitement, and each time with different details. His exuberance was always contagious. Around Bryan, you couldn't help but smile.

On top of his joyful personality, Bryan was passionate. Something would ignite his interest, and he would spend weeks learning everything there was to know about it. This translated into large collections of the most random things. Shoes, old sewing machines, and antique Sunbeam MixMasters lay scattered around their house. Bryan could recount a story about each item.

None of Bryan's collections, however, rivaled that of his ukuleles. Bryan played the ukulele in the worship band in church. This began a passion for the instrument which resulted in a vast collection. He would buy them from all over- broken, scraped, worn, it did not matter. Bryan would take them into his home and lovingly restore the ones he could. One year, he was so excited about his hobby that all his neighbors received a ukulele from the Holcombes for Christmas.

Karla was very patient with his collections. She took the most random assortments of them and made them beautiful. While normally, an entire shelf of Sunbeam MixMasters would be unusual in a home, when Karla placed her hands on them, arranging them beautifully and lovingly, they would become a gorgeous, eccentric, museum-worthy display. The most beautiful of her creations also lay in Bryan's unused ukuleles. The instruments that were damaged beyond repair, Karla transformed into birdhouses that hung peacefully in the trees around their home. They were filled with nests and singing birds.

This is the way it was with the Holcombes. Everything they touched turned into something absolutely beautiful and full of love.

Their family will always remember long days spent playing games, eating good food, making messes with water balloons, and eating too much sugar. A favorite event was always the white elephant gift exchange. The gifts were never serious, always gag presents which would make everyone smile- presents such as a box of used soda cans, an old pair of shoes, or most importantly a can of expired, decade-old snails. This was the coveted trophy of the Holcombe family, the one everyone playfully argued over. Each year, it ended up in the exchange, along with the rest of the random knick-knacks. Each year, the person who went home triumphant would keep it at their house, only to bring it back and trade it all over again.

Anyone and everyone was welcomed into the Holcombe family. It didn't matter how broken, scraped or worn they were: once the Holcombes got a hold of you, their intense love and deep abiding faith began to slowly transform life into something beautiful.

Bryan and Karla Holcombe joined their Father in Heaven that morning, after 40 wonderful years of marriage, in the church they loved deeply. They had been members of the First Baptist Church of Sutherland Springs for 13 years.

* * *

Julie ran from the nursery, taking a sharp turn around the side of the building, bursting into the fellowship hall. She searched the cabinets and shelves for anything which could be used to tourniquet Zach's wounds. Once again, there were no rags. She sprinted from the building, toward the parking lot, urgency driving her forward.

Her last chance was her car. Inside, she found a box full of them. She dragged it inside as quickly as she could and attended to Zachary.

Julie made eye contact with Zachary as she knelt beside him. She could see the pain in his eyes. But the boy was brave, brave beyond his years. He was not screaming or crying. In fact, the church was silent. There were no cries from the wounded. Just eerie silence.

"I know you have to move me," Zachary told her. "And I know it's going to hurt. Please just do what you have to."

Julie did. She bound up his wounds and did her best to stop the bleeding. When she was finished, she moved on to the next person.

At some point, amidst the binding, bandages, and blood, she noticed something in the rafters of the church. She paused for a moment and looked up. Above her, was a radiant, white cloud.

Gun smoke, people try to tell her. Julie, you saw gun smoke. Or debris.

But it wasn't gun smoke, or debris.

It was the adrenaline, Julie. Nothing more than the adrenaline and fear.

But it wasn't adrenaline, or fear.

You were in shock, Julie. It was just shock.

But that wasn't it either.

Because before Julie's eyes, she watched the souls of 26 people ascend into Heaven. She watched the moment each one of them entered the kingdom of God. And suddenly, her fear was gone. A peace which truly passes all understanding enveloped her. She knew they were at rest. She knew they were safe in the arms of Christ. So, turning back to the task at hand, Julie continued attending to the survivors, binding bullet wounds with rough, bloodstained towels and moving on to the next person as quickly as she was able, whispering fervent prayers for strength as she moved. So methodical and desperate were Julie's actions and attention, that she didn't even hear the sirens as they drew ever closer.

✣ ✣ ✣

Hank slammed on his brakes at the side of the church, speeding in next to Mike Marr, a Wilson County Sheriff Deputy. As they spilled out of their cars, Hank gripped his personal AR-15 tightly, his teeth bared as he made eye contact with his sergeant and with the Deputy. Another car braked next to them, and Texas Game Warden Rob Frets leapt out.

They turned toward the church, falling quickly into a four-man contact group. There was a fence around a small playground, and a side door to the church lay slightly ajar. Hank led the group around the fence, the Deputy at his heels. The Sergeant, Donald Keil, made up the rear with the Game Warden. Hank stepped through the door, his AR-15 at the ready.

* * *

The two police cars that came screeching into town, barreling toward the Baptist Church, broke the silent tension in Rusty's car. They shattered his illusion of a benign morning. They braked hard on the shoulder of the highway, near the side of the small, white church. Rusty and his son watched as three officers jumped out of the cars, armed with AR-15s and bulletproof vests.

It was at the church, then.

Rusty glanced at his son. He had to keep him safe. But he was also on call. He was close, and his experience could be the difference between life and death in this situation.

Rusty stepped on the gas and rushed toward the church.

* * *

As soon as Hank stepped through the door, he could already smell it: the acrid scent of gunpowder, and blood. The smell choked the air of the small office adjacent to the chapel.

Hank did not pause, but pushed forward, stepping past a bookcase, a couch, and a desk, moving toward the door which led to the chapel listening for any noise that could signal what he was walking into.

There was no noise. Ahead was a total absence of noise. Completely, and utterly silent. As Hank stepped through the door to the chapel, blinking through the haze of gun smoke and debris, he saw the first casualty. If it were not for his years of training, Hank would have frozen at the horrific scene before him. But he was trained for this.

"Let me see your hands!" Hank cried, striding forward into the church. "Let me see your hands!"

Hands shot up hesitantly all over the church as the men combed through the sanctuary, passing by splintered pews, guns raised. Hank searched through the groups of wounded and fallen congregants for an armed assailant, unsure if they would be ambushed from behind a pew or from one of the groups of huddled survivors.

The damage was complete. Shattered glass scattered across the floor, mixing with splintered chunks of wood and too much blood.

"Julie put your hands up," Hank heard a girl call.

In the corner, a busy blonde woman in a black dress was bent over, bloodied rags clutched in her hands. She didn't seem to hear.

"Julie," the girl called again, louder this time to get her attention.

A Town Called Sutherland Springs

Julie looked up hastily at the sound of Morgan's familiar voice, dropping the rags and raising hands which were covered in blood.

"He's gone," someone said. "The shooter's gone."

Hank lowered his gun, handing it off to one of the other officers, and sprang into action. Julie, the woman in the corner, turned back to the wounded woman in front of her. Hank strode forward, approaching a small girl who lay huddled beneath a pew, dazed, her clothes stained scarlet, her hair stuck to her forehead. He scooped her up in his arms and ran for the front door, calling out to the others for help as he leapt over debris and broken pews.

✷ ✷ ✷

As Rusty pulled into the church parking lot, he could tell the threat was over. It was unbelievably quiet as he turned off the ignition to his truck.

"Stay in the car," he told Jase as he threw open the door and leapt out.

He didn't wait for his son to respond. He rushed forward, approaching the small, white building with growing dread. An officer stumbled outside; a little girl clutched in his arms.

"Victims inside! Go!" he shouted.

Rusty followed orders. As he crossed over the threshold of the small church, stepping through the large, wooden double doors which hung open, splintered and riddled with bullet holes, he choked in shock and came to a horrified halt.

"Oh, God," he whispered.

Chapter Six: Gunpowder and Blood

The first thing which penetrated Rusty's confused and shock-riddled brain was the smell.

Gunpowder. Gunpowder and blood.

The smell permeated the air. It filled up all his senses until it seemed to consume him. It took a moment before he could process anything else.

The next thing he saw was the dust, the blood, and the bodies. The pews were splintered. Bullets had ripped through the wood and scattered it across the carpet, ricocheted off the ground, and ripped up whole patches of concrete. The windows were shattered. Everything was destroyed. Gun smoke clung to the air in a thick fog. And the people- the people were all still.

They're all dead, he thought, looking around at the people who lay on the ground. All of them. They are all dead.

It was a moment before Rusty realized that he was walking, like a ghost or a zombie up the middle aisle, toward the front of the church. He barely realized he had moved. The silence in the church was almost deafening. It filled him with panic. This couldn't be happening. All his training, all his years of experience- it had not prepared him for this. Never had he thought he would walk into a scene ripped straight from a war zone. This was Sutherland Springs for God's sake!

When he reached the pulpit, Rusty turned and faced down the church with a growing numbness. He had to act. Surely, someone was left alive.

He couldn't do it like this. He had to start somewhere. He had to have a process. It took a few moments before the horror gripping Rusty's soul faded just enough that his seventeen years of experience as a paramedic was able to click into place. When it did, Rusty rushed to the back of the church- pushing his fear down to a place that he would doubtlessly need to revisit later- and began systematically checking pulses.

In the back rows, it was easy to tell that most of the people had already passed. Rusty tried not to focus on their faces as he rushed from person to person, skipping over the people whose eyes were open and glassy. It wasn't until the fifth row that he found someone.

It was a woman, hunched over in the pew. He bent down and checked her pulse. She was gone. He tried not to look at the little girl next to her. She was gone too. He didn't need to check her pulse to know.

As he turned to continue up the aisle, something grabbed his ankle. He looked down, to see a tiny little hand reaching out from under the woman.

The hand was pale, and incredibly small. Too small. How could it be so small?

It gripped his pant leg tightly though, with a strength that belied its size.

He moved quickly, bending down and shifting the woman to the side. There, shielded beneath her, was a little boy.

***

Rusty had become a volunteer firefighter and paramedic after coming upon a car crash with two of his friends. It was in Corpus Christi. The car had rolled multiple times, and they were the first to drive past the scene. Inside the wrecked car was a friend of theirs from high school. The three men panicked. They had no idea what to do. Together, they reached inside the car and dragged their friend out.

When the fire department arrived at the scene, they admonished Rusty and his friends. Dragging their friend out of the car had been the wrong thing to do. But they hadn't known what else to do.

So, they watched from the sidelines as EMS administered first aid and loaded their friend into the ambulance. They hated the helplessness they had felt at the scene. They hated not knowing what to do and felt useless.

Rusty and his friends swore they wouldn't feel that way again next time a situation like this occurred. They would be prepared, and properly trained. So, seventeen years before Rusty stepped into the church in Sutherland Springs to find a little boy barely clinging to life, Rusty finished his training as a paramedic.

✳ ✳ ✳

Rusty moved the woman aside as quickly and as gently as he could. There, beneath her, was a little boy. He was so small, so still, and so fragile that for a moment, Rusty wasn't sure if he was alive. Then, he saw his eyes. They were half open, watching him. His little hands flexed.

Rusty scooped him up, gently and firmly. He had to get him out of the church, out of the dim light and dust, and out of the choking smell of blood and gun smoke. He had to get him in the sunlight, where he could assess the damage. Cradling him against his chest, Rusty turned and rushed from the building, stepping over debris as he went.

Stepping out of the church was like stepping onto a foreign planet. It was such a different scene. The sun was shining. There were barely any clouds in the sky. It could have been any Sunday, at any small church, in any town in Texas.

Rushing over the concrete sidewalk and into the short, yellowing grass of the lawn, Rusty knelt and started to work. Using his pocketknife, he cut off the little boy's clothes. There was so much blood, and he didn't have his paramedic bag. All he had was his belt.

He took it off and wrapped it around the boy's leg, pulling it tight to make a tourniquet. The boy was shot six times. He had to stop the bleeding.

✳ ✳ ✳

Joann was a thirty-year-old mother of three and stepmother of one. You couldn't tell the difference, though.

She raised and treated Ryland as her own son. Her eldest daughter, Rihanna, and second daughter Emily were from a different relationship. When she married Chris, she inherited Ryland, and together, they had Brooke. Joann was a generous, loving woman. She was everyone's best friend and was always there for people. She was joyful, sincere, and dedicated. Joann loved to help people, and often went out of her way to meet everyone else's needs.

Joann was a proper country girl. She loved blue jeans, horses, country music, and cowgirl boots. She always wore the same tan boots, which were beat up and worn from years of use. Like any self-respecting country girl, she had two big dogs that she adored. She loved animals and kept a coop of chickens. Joann always spent long hours outdoors, taking care of the chickens or watching the kids play outside. She would sit on the porch as the sun set, casting beautiful warm tones of pink and orange across the darkening sky, talking for hours with Sandy, her mother-in-law as the kids played on bikes and scooters or ran through the yard wildly.

Joann loved her children and was fiercely protective of them. Each day, she made sure to spend time with each one, individually. She would cuddle them on the couch, tickle them, chase them around, and most importantly, let each one know how important they were, and how much they were loved. She was very involved in their lives. Joann was always the first one to volunteer for school field trips or stay up into the late hours of the night helping her children perfect their school projects.

Although conflict rarely occurred, if it did, no one wanted to get between Joann and her kids. She was a mama bear, and would defend them, and protect them above all else. This fierceness was an extension of Joann's overwhelming love for her children. She would do anything for them. Her family was her world.

The Ward family was very close. One of their favorite activities was to go to Palmetto State Park and swim in the lake. They would pack up picnics of sandwiches, chips, fruit, and a cooler full of soda, and head out, strapping life jackets on the youngest, and slathering up with sunscreen. The children would run down the rough pier at full speed and leap into the sparkling water below. They would swim together for hours, laughter broken by splashing waves and lilting voices. Joann, Chris, and Sandy had to practically drag them out of the water when it was time to eat. Many days each year passed this way, Joann, Chris, and Sandy swimming as the children wildly leapt from the pier, ignoring splinters and weeds, covered in the mud from the bottom of the lake, sun-kissed and blissfully happy.

Emily Garcia, Joann's second daughter, was seven years old. Although she was a shy and quiet child, and had a habit of drawing into herself, Emily loved people and wanted to be friends with everyone. Like her mother, she was very passionate about others and incredibly helpful. Emily went out of her way to do the hard chores that no one else wanted to do, striving to make everyone's life a bit easier.

Emily's best friend was she was seven-year-old Haley, Sandy's daughter. They shared a birthday and were as close as sisters. Haley often came over to play. They would pretend they were cats, crawling around the yard, meowing at each other, and chasing balls of yarn. They would lounge in the sun and pretend to clean their fur, purring happily as they imagined. Emily loved animals.

When Emily grew up, she wanted to be a teacher. This may have stemmed from the joy she got from teaching her best friend how to ride a bike. Once she learned, they would ride their bikes up and down their dead-end road, with Ryland and Brooke chasing behind them on scooters.

She was a playful, creative girl. Her artistic creations were proudly displayed all throughout the Ward household. Emily spent many hours bent over paper, crayons and markers clutched in her hands, drawing new pictures for her friends, her grandmother, her aunt, and her mother and stepfather.

Brooke was five years old. She was a streak of color, frilly skirts, and exuberance. A proper princess, Brooke liked nothing better than pretty dresses and jewelry. Brooke could often be seen dancing, twirling throughout the house to an imaginary tune, the folds of her skirt billowing out around her as she spun. She was going to be a ballerina.

Brooke was opinionated and loved attention. The spotlight easily found her: her grace and bubbly personality were contagious. If questioned, it is doubtful that Brooke could have picked a favorite princess. She loved them all and knew all their names. After all, she was a princess in her own right- her parents adored her. Her father, Chris, would do anything for her. It wasn't uncommon for him to leave the house at ten o'clock at night for a grocery run because Brooke had bounded into their room, her sweet little voice and perfect smile requesting cupcakes. Her father could never resist that smile and those big, bright eyes.

Brooke loved other children, and was very close with her brother, Ryland. She worshipped Emily, Haley, and Rihanna, and followed them everywhere, her little legs struggling to keep up with them. No matter how girly she was, Brooke loved to play outside. She loved swimming, bubble baths, and dolls.

She was a Daddy's girl. November 4th, as Chris got ready for work, Brooke followed him around and filled his pockets full of small trinkets. Little, chubby toddler hands stuffed in small toys, bits of debris, and scribbles, while she hummed and chased her daddy around the house.

"What're you doing?" Chris asked her as he paused to pull on his shoes.

"Daddy, I'm giving you stuff, so you remember me," she responded with her signature smile.

Later, after the news of the shooting reached Chris, he would rush to the hospital to pace anxiously in the waiting room for any news- news of his son, news of his girls. News of his wife. November 5th was their anniversary. That day, they would have celebrated six years of marriage. In his exhaustion when he got off work and collapsed into bed, Chris hadn't even had the chance to wish Joann a happy anniversary.

As he paced in the hospital, the harsh clinical light almost blinding him, the doctors rushing about from room to room, he wondered if he would ever get the chance to tell her. Chris crammed his hands in his pockets and found the gifts from Brooke still waiting for him there. Gifts placed by a child's hands so she would always be remembered. As if her smile and warm hugs were not enough.

Rihanna, Emily, Ryland, and Brooke typically attended First Baptist Church of Sutherland Springs with Sandy and Haley. That morning, Sandy and her husband stayed behind. Joann, who had just begun attending church with her children, took the kids instead. Though she hadn't attended long, she had already begun to consider the congregation to be her family.

When the shooting broke out, Joann turned to her children. Zach Poston, after being shielded by his grandmother, Peggy, kicked Rihanna under a pew and fell in front of her, guarding her from the shots. Joann, knowing Rihanna was safe, threw herself on top of her other three children, wrapping them all in her arms and using herself as a human shield. Her sacrifice saved Ryland, allowing Rusty Duncan enough time to pull the child to safety.

Emily and Brooke had been members of First Baptist Church of Sutherland Springs for a little over a year, and Joann had only been to two Sunday services before they passed away together and met again at the gates of Heaven.

***

An ambulance pulled up into the yellowing lawn of the church, the lights spinning in a dizzying array of colors. Eagle Creek was emblazoned on the side. As paramedics spilled from the vehicle, Rusty shouted for a medic bag. One was in his hands in moments. Opening the bag, he pulled more tourniquets and began tying off the boy's arm. More ambulances arrived, followed by more people, rushing over the lawn in flurries of motion, swirling lights, and screaming sirens. None of it mattered. Rusty's whole world was now this boy- this little, tiny boy who somehow still clung to life. This little boy who he would not let die today.

As the EMS arrived, paramedics began to rush over the scene, hauling up the 22 survivors and packing them into screaming ambulances and helicopters. Julie was able to take a step back. Covered in blood, wounded, and yet calmer than she would have thought possible, Julie finally took the time to call her husband.

"I need you to come to the church," she told him. "There has been a shooting. I am ok, but Kris has been shot."

She didn't tell him Kyle was still missing. She wanted him to be able to make it to church in one piece.

✶ ✶ ✶

Later, Julie would find out that the killer had emptied his magazine to stop Kyle. While the killer had methodically worked his way up the aisle, Kyle had crept backwards toward the door. Once he passed where the killer was, he stood and ran. Fear and desperation pumping action into his shaking limbs, Kyle stood and leapt over the pews, flying past the fallen congregants, and making a break for the double doors of the church. The killer saw him and turned, firing a barrage of bullets after him. As the bullets buried themselves in the wall, chipping off drywall and shattering what glass was left intact, Kyle scrambled over the pews and squeezed underneath the final one before bursting out of the church into the blinding sunlight. The door smacked hard on his shoulder and rebounded against the wall as he ran, taking a sharp left and rounding the side of the church.

He had to get help. He had to call someone. He had to get the police here. His family, his fiancée, they were all counting on him.

He ran faster than he ever had before, around the church into the field as the gunfire continued behind him. The grass wound up around his ankles, threatening to trip him. The uneven ground, weeds, and shifting sand of the field behind the church couldn't stop him, though. He barely looked as he bolted across Highway 87, ran through the parking lot, and collapsed against the door of the Valero gas station. His hands smacked against the glass, pushing a door which was locked tight, his eyes wide and manic.

"Help!" he screamed. "Someone is shooting up the church! My family is in there! Someone help! Call 911!"

It took a moment for the people in the gas station to unlock the door. When they heard the gunfire, they had locked it and crouched behind the counter, unsure from which direction the gunfire originated. When they saw Kyle running, clad in black, covered in debris, and streaked with blood, they had assumed the worst. But at the sound of his desperate cries, one of the employees stood and unlocked the door.

Kyle spilled into the gas station, the adrenaline which had fueled his shaking legs finally giving out as he fell to the ground.

"Please, someone call 911," he gasped. "Someone help them."

It was a few hours later when the family found each other again. When they reunited, they headed to the hospital and spent the following days in the waiting room as doctors worked tirelessly on Kris. Eventually, months later, they would all be together again at home, with Kris released from the hospital against seemingly insurmountable odds. Kyle would marry his fiancée, Morgan, who was also present in the church during the shooting. The ceremony would be beautiful and filled with hope, laughter, and love. All of this was to come in the days, weeks, and months that followed that horrible Sunday.

But for now, as Julie's husband, Kip, rushed toward the church and ambulances came and went, Kyle was missing, Kris was being rushed to the hospital, and Julie stood, helplessly, waiting for any news of her beloved sons.

* * *

Matt pulled the car into the driveway in time to see Pam rushing around the corner of the house, up toward the church, quick on the heels of Stephanie. He turned to his wife and saw the fear and panic in her eyes.

"Go," he told her. "I'll take care of the dogs. Just go."

"Thank you," she cried as she threw the door open, barely waiting for the car to stop before bolting out of it and sprinting down the road after her mother.

Matt's hands shook as he clipped the leashes onto the dogs and started to rush them inside.

A Town Called Sutherland Springs

✷ ✷ ✷

Matt's first impression of Rachel's family was overwhelming. He had never experienced a family quite so loud. They didn't yell at each other necessarily, they just all had a lot to say and weren't afraid to say it, even if they were across the house from each other. They talked, laughed, and constantly harassed one another. There was always noise in the house, whether it was conversation, music, or the blare of the TV. There didn't seem to be a moment of silence to hold onto.

He didn't know why he expected anything different, though. Rachel was much the same. She was opinionated and unashamed to let people know exactly what she thought. At first, he had found her exuberance and outspoken nature exhausting. Then, slowly, she had grown on him until his feelings had turned from annoyance to something else entirely. The more time he spent with her, the more he liked her fearless nature, her unshakable faith, and her dark sense of humor.

When he asked her out on a date, he hadn't expected the condition she gave him. It turned out that although she liked him too, she didn't date anyone unless they first asked her father for permission. It was a family tradition, she explained. And family was incredibly important to Rachel, as well as her father's approval.

So, when he first walked into the Willeford house in Sutherland Springs, to ask for permission to date Rachel, he shouldn't have been surprised at the noise but somehow he was anyway. The family greeted him like an old friend, opening the door to a house that was warm, messy, and loud. Loud and full of love, just like the family themselves.

Stephen, Rachel's father, seemed imposing. He wasn't particularly tall, but he was built like a brick wall, had a long-grizzled beard which covered most of his face, and had wild, long, graying hair that stuck up about him like a wiry bush. He wore a Harley-Davidson shirt and carried himself with a confidence which was intimidating.

"Don't worry," Rachel had said. "He may look scary, but my dad is a big teddy bear. He is excited to meet you."

Worried? Not worried, really. Just intimidated. He had never had to ask for permission to date a girl before. He wasn't even really sure what to say, or how to broach the topic. This girl was worth it, though, so he had to figure out how, no matter how awkward it was.

When he finally did ask permission, Stephen simply asked him if he liked camping.

"Camping?"

"Yes, camping. Do you want to go camping with me?"

Rachel had warned him this might happen. But even so, it surprised him.

So that is what brought him to this. This campground at Inks Lake State Park with a man who was nearly a stranger to him, and this rocky cliffside, 30 feet above the cool, sparkling water, barefoot and in his swim trunks. Inks Lake stretched below him in a great, blue mass, the water reflecting shiny points of the bright, Texas sun into his eyes. Around them, scrubby bushes and trees grew from the craggy rocks of the cliff, and the near-stifling heat was made just tolerable by a soft, summer breeze. Stephen grinned at him, his wild, grey hair sticking up around him in a chaotic halo and his large, squarish feet digging into the rocks.

"I'm not jumping until you jump," Matt told him, not believing Rachel's father had coaxed him up here.

It looked a lot higher now that he was up here, staring at the waves lapping against the rocks. Looking down from the cliff made his head spin. But Matt was no coward. He wasn't going to back down now.

"Well, I'm not going until you go. So, you want to go together?"

"We could hold hands," Matt responded teasingly.

"Sounds good to me," Stephen answered, reaching out and gripping Matt with a calloused square hand.

What the hell, Matt conceded, and together they leapt from the cliff.

Matt didn't know it, but when Stephen came home from the camping trip, he pulled his daughter aside.

"You're going to marry that boy someday, Rachel," he told her. "You don't know it yet, but just watch. You're going to marry him."

* * *

Rachel ran after her mother's retreating back, up to her neighbor's house where her sister stood in shock.

The ground seemed to spin out of control, like the whirling lights of an ambulance as she took in the scene before her.

The doors of the church were thrown open, but it was dark inside. Bullet holes tore through the church's white, pristine paint. Churchgoers littered the front lawn in various stages of undress, crying, panting, bleeding.

There were a few police cars and ambulances already there. EMS rushed over the lawn, in and out of the church, flitting back and forth with bandages, water bottles, and bloodied gauze. There weren't enough of them. Such a little town was not equipped for this.

A silent scream built up in Rachel's chest as she watched the scene- a scream which seemed to only build and build, the vocal cords tensing, the muscles clenching, but with no release from it. No release from the endless, building terror. Her eyes searched the ground, searched the injured, searched the few onlookers, searched the ambulances for her father.

"Pam," a familiar voice called.

Pam, Stephanie, and Rachel turned toward the voice as one. There stood Kathleen, their neighbor.

"Kathleen," Pam said. "Where is my husband?"

"He went after the son of a bitch," responded Kathleen's husband, Fred.

His eager, round face glistened with anger. "He shot him and then went after him."

"Went after him?" Pam responded. "In which direction?"

"He left his phone at home," Stephanie whispered in horror, the knowledge sinking in that her father was truly missing.

Fred shrugged, but began to point out the bullet casings on the ground, the holes in his truck where the killer had returned fire, and the shattered windshield where a bullet had grazed past where her father had stood.

"How did he go after him?"

"Some truck," Fred responded. "The bastard drove off, and Stephen jumped in some truck and took off after him."

"Was he hurt? Did he get shot?" Pam asked urgently.

Fred didn't answer. He didn't know.

"God, please say he is ok. I know he'll be ok. He has to be," Rachel croaked, her voice barely audible.

✷ ✷ ✷

"With a terrible cry the Balrog fell forward, and its shadow plunged down and vanished. But even as it fell it swung its whip, and the thongs lashed and curled about the wizard's knees, dragging him to the brink. He staggered and fell, grasped vainly at the stone, and slid into the abyss. 'Fly, you fools!' he cried, and was gone."[2]

Shocked silence filled the small Saturn as Pam paused to let the words sink in.

It was a Willeford family tradition for Pam to read aloud on car trips. This was one of the habits developed to keep the three young children captivated, and out of each other's faces, during the hour-long trips into town. Because of this, the children had learned from a very young age to love books. They had spent hours in the car, listening to their mother's soft voice read many stories, stories of wizards, a

---

[2] J.R.R. Tolkien "The Fellowship of the Ring."

wardrobe, sign-seekers, and pig keepers. Stories which captured the children's imagination.

The only noise heard in the car for a few moments was the soft whisper of the air conditioner and the rhythmic thumping of the road beneath the tires. Then, the kids erupted.

"Mom, did Gandalf just die?" Stephanie exclaimed.

Blake, who was sitting in the middle seat between his two sisters, began to whimper. Although he was only five, he had grown to love Gandalf during their time in Middle Earth. He had traveled with him, the band of dwarves, and little Bilbo as they confronted Smaug, the terrible fire-breathing dragon. He had been excited to learn that there were more books, more books in which the wizard with the grand fireworks would embark on another adventure. Now, he was as devastated as Frodo and the Fellowship at Gandalf's apparent demise.

"No," Rachel, the 7-year-old middle sister proclaimed. "He isn't dead."

"He just fell into the abyss with the Balrog," Pam responded from the front seat, glancing over at her husband, who was driving.

Blake began to cry.

"No, mom, you don't understand," Rachel responded, frustrated. "He isn't dead. I know he isn't. He can't be."

"Why?" Pam asked.

"Because he is Gandalf, Mom. Just watch. I don't know what is happening. But I know he can't be dead. The writer is trying to trick us. I won't fall for it. He isn't dead."

"Blake, stop crying," Stephanie, who was nine years old and simply knew she was more sensible than her siblings, grumbled irritably. "It's just a book. Calm down."

"B-b-bu-," Blake began blubbering incoherently.

"Blake, he isn't dead," Rachel insisted resolutely. "Really, he can't have died. Just watch. He can't be dead. He's Gandalf."

Pam gave another sideways glance to Stephen, sharing a small smile with him which the children were too busy arguing with each other to see.

"He fell off a cliff, Rachel," Stephanie said with exasperation, trying to hide her own despair beneath a mask of indifference.

Blake continued to cry between the two arguing girls, who leaned over him slightly as they fought.

"I don't care!" Rachel retorted. "A cliff can't kill Gandalf! Just watch! I know I'm right. He isn't dead. You just don't understand!"

"Stop arguing!" Pam announced, reopening the old paperback, and once again finding her place. "I guess we'll just have to see, won't we?"

The girls leaned back as Blake sniffled pathetically. Rachel crossed her arms and looked out the window as the countryside sped past. They would see soon. They would see she was right. Gandalf would be back. She was sure of it.

* * *

"We're after him, he's going down 539."

The young man spoke quickly into his phone. I glanced at my companion, examining him for a moment. He was a long, lanky young man, wearing a large, tan, felt cowboy hat with a turquoise and red beaded band, a large, striped feather sticking out of it. He wore a bright orange undershirt with a tan, western button up, blue jeans, and as any country boy would, a large belt and belt buckle. He looked to be in his late twenties and was covered in tattoos. At the top of his throat, right beneath his chin, a longhorn skull rested, the inked black horns wrapping around the sides of his neck, branching up toward his ears. The stranger had calm, brown eyes, brown hair, and a southern accent that sounded nonchalant and polite. A toothpick rested in the corner of his mouth, and as he spoke to the operator on the phone, the thin sliver of wood moved back and forth, switching from corner to corner. One of his hands was slung across the steering wheel, the other holding his cell phone to his ear as he sped down the highway, flying around curves and overtaking cars, passing one after another as the speedometer climbed higher and higher.

I was thankful that he had his cellphone and was already in contact with 911. In my haste to leave my house, I left mine behind.

For a brief moment, I thought about my family and worried about what would happen if I didn't make it home. I thought about my cellphone, buzzing with calls from my friends, my family, and my wife, trying to reach me to find out what was going on. Then, I thought of all the people in the church, whose phones were no doubt already going off as news of the shooting reached their loved ones. I thought of all

A Town Called Sutherland Springs

the calls that would never be answered, and scrubbed thoughts of my own cell phone from my mind.

I clattered and bounced wildly in the seat as we careened down the highway, passing bewildered Sunday morning drivers in a blur. As my companion explained our current whereabouts to the 911 operator, giving live, second by second updates, my hands brushed across the rifle and pressed the rough button to drop the magazine. It slid from my firearm, into my waiting hand.

There was only one round left in the magazine. It glistened in the sun for a moment, as I stared at it. The metal felt cold in my hands as I crammed the magazine back into the rifle. There was only one round left in the magazine, and one in the chamber. I only had two bullets left.

Better make these count.

"We're going about 90," the young man responded to the operator. "We don't see him yet."

I had driven down this road so many times before. I wondered if it had always been so long as we flew across the bridge over the Cibolo Creek; the creek where my kids and I fished when they were little, where my daughter's eyes had nearly popped out of her skull in surprise when we wrenched the biggest catfish I had ever seen off a hook, and folded it into a cooler- or was adrenaline and fear stretching it out into eternity, making this road turn into some sort of hellish purgatory?

"You know if you catch up to him, you're probably going to have to run him off the road," I said gruffly, turning my eyes again to my new companion.

The young man nodded, as oddly calm in appearance as I had been at the church.

"I already figured as much," he responded, moving the toothpick to the other side of his mouth.

He glanced in my direction, his phone still held to his ear, his arm nonchalantly thrown across the wheel as if chasing another car at upwards of 90 mph was an everyday occurrence for him.

Time passed too slowly. I could hear the blood roaring in my ears, could feel every groove and texture of the firearm locked in my hands. Every inch of my body was alert and tense as I stared through the windshield, the road stretching and growing before us. No matter how fast we drove, it wasn't fast enough. Energy fueled by fear and adrenaline kept me upright as the countryside sped by our windows, passing River Oaks Baptist Church, passing the Polley Mansion, passing the place on the road where my parents were killed by a drunk driver.

As we rounded another curve, the truck careening so wildly that I had to let go of my rifle with one hand to steady myself against the door, we saw the retreating back end and shattered window of the killer's car down the road, ahead of us.

"We see him!" my companion barked to the operator, momentarily breaking his composure, and leaning forward in his seat. "We're coming up on his tail. Passing County Road 2772."

I gripped my gun again, ready, teeth grinding down tight.

A Town Called Sutherland Springs

I only had two shots left. Only God knew how many he had. It didn't matter, though. One way or another, this would end with a shootout. Whether that was with me or the police, I didn't know. All I knew was that I was here, and capable, and someone had to do something.

The car ahead drove erratically, hesitantly, swerving. Suddenly it slowed, and pulled off the highway, the tires bouncing across the shoulder of the country road, coming to a dramatic halt.

The young man slammed on his brakes. I braced my legs in the floorboard of his truck to keep myself from crashing forward, and gripped the handle of the door, readying my rifle and throwing the door open before we came to a complete stop. My rifle ahead of me, my leg hanging out over open space, I started to jump from the truck. Before my feet hit the pavement, the Explorer lurched forward suddenly. It bounced roughly across the grass and jumped back onto the highway, smashing into a bright, yellow street sign, which folded and flipped over the top of the vehicle as if it was made of paper. The sign, a warning of a coming curve, bounced in the grass as the vehicle recklessly lurched around the curve.

My tattooed companion didn't hesitate, but gunned the engine again, speeding after him. I pushed off the truck's step, propelling myself back into the passenger's seat, and slammed the door closed behind me. Ahead, as we rounded the curve, we watched the Explorer swerve erratically, run off the highway, and fly into a field. It tore through a barbed wire fence, bounding into the long grass before coming to a sudden halt.

The truck slammed to a stop again, both of us lurching forward with the momentum. I threw open the door.

"Stay down," I called out, leaping onto the street. "Stay down below the dash!"

* * *

Across the street from the church, Rachel watched as a paramedic worked over the still form of a boy. She turned away for a moment, whispering desperate prayers which had no form or direction under her breath, and looked at Kathleen's house, her eyes needing a break from the bodies strewn across the lawn. It was then that Rachel noticed the other two people on Kathleen's porch.

An elderly Hispanic man sat with his back against the wall, on the steps of the porch, pressing a towel against his leg. The blood was visible.

The second nearly brought her to her knees. There, leaning against the man, was a little girl. A black, swelling bruise was forming on her forehead. Her blonde hair was matted and stuck to her face, stained dark red and tangled with flesh. Her bright blue shirt was covered in crimson as well, her black leggings sticky down to her shoes. She sat, unmoving, her bright blue eyes staring and dazed. Kathleen sat behind her, rubbing her back and whispering. The little girl did not show any sign that she was aware of Kathleen's attention.

* * *

"Ryland is over there," Rusty heard a woman say.

A man appeared then, hovering over Rusty and the boy. He was in sheer panic, eyes wide and belligerent.

"They killed my son!" he yelled, standing over the still boy. "They killed my son!"

The man began to chatter, ranting in panic and fear, his grip on reality spinning out of control.

"He's not dead!" Rusty yelled. "Get down here and talk to him! He's not dead!"

The man continued to blabber, swaying back and forth, and pacing and screaming.

"He hears you!" Rusty said again. "Everything you are saying, he hears! Get down here and talk to him!"

His father knelt. "You have to calm down," Rusty spoke quickly as he worked. "Keep your son awake."

The boy's eyes started to close. His father let out a strangled noise.

"No, Ryland, don't you go to sleep!" Rusty screamed, his hands working fast to stop the bleeding and stabilize the boy. "Ryland, wake up and stay with me!"

Ryland's eyes fluttered and opened just a bit. Rusty continued to yell at him as he worked, doing everything he could to slow the bleeding. When Ryland's eyes would begin to drift shut again, dazed and exhausted, Rusty would yell. He wasn't sure how long he was there, hunched over the small figure of the child, hands slick with his blood, wrapping bandages and tourniquets while chaos erupted around him. It had to have been only a few minutes. But to Rusty, it was an entire lifetime. Everything he had trained for was for this moment. For this day. For this little boy. He could not die. Not today.

"We got to move him now, we got to go!" Rusty finally said, turning to Ryland's father.

Together, they lifted the child off the ground and carried him to a waiting ambulance. With the help of a paramedic, they loaded him onto the vehicle.

"Go!" Rusty shouted as the paramedic slammed the doors shut. "Get out of here!"

As the ambulance raced away to where helicopters waited to airlift victims to San Antonio, Rusty gave himself one moment to stare after the little boy.

Then, he turned, took a deep breath, and rushed back into the church.

Chapter Seven: The Longest Seven Minutes

Minutes passed. They felt like hours.

Matt joined Rachel as EMS hauled a little boy with an oxygen mask strapped to his face onto a stretcher. The boy was bleeding and naked. Matt's hand tightened around Rachel's shoulder as she finally sat, the spinning world becoming too much as the ambulance screamed away, and the sound of a helicopter's blades sliced through the air.

How could this happen? Surely this was not real. Surely this was just a nightmare.

Rachel sat for only a moment; her face buried in her hands. There had to be something she could do. She couldn't just sit here. Standing again, shakily, she turned toward the porch where the little girl sat.

Kathleen still sat behind the girl, stroking her back, whispering to her. But her voice was shaking now. The brave woman was getting overwhelmed. They made eye contact as Rachel approached the porch, a lump in her throat.

"Ms. Rachel," Kathleen spoke, her voice strained, and her eyes lost as she introduced the girl. "She is homeschooled."

The girl barely moved. Rachel watched for only a moment before she fought the tears away and pasted on a smile.

"Really?" she responded, stepping forward, kneeling in front of the little girl. "So was I! That is so amazing!"

She talked to the little girl for the next few minutes, struggling to keep the fear and the strain from her voice. She asked her how old she was. She was seven. Rachel asked about her family, her life, her favorite movie, her pets.

She looked at Kathleen and mouthed a question as the girl responded that Moana was her favorite movie.

"Her mother?" Rachel mouthed silently.

Tears spilled over onto Kathleen's cheeks, and she shook her head.

Oh, God.

Time passed as Rachel and Kathleen fought to keep the girl awake, fought to keep the fear and horror from overwhelming them. As Rachel, Matt, Pam, and Stephanie struggled not to think about where Stephen was, and if he was all right.

EMS told Kathleen they couldn't see the child. Not yet at least. There were others whose injuries were far worse.

Keep her awake, they said. Don't let her fall asleep.

So they kept her awake as the chaos of the scene continued swelling around them. Rachel sang songs from Moana. They talked about her family. Learned about her various cats. Kathleen held her hair back as the little girl vomited, and Rachel steadied her as she swayed on her feet. Time passed in a terrible crawl which seemed never-ending.

* * *

It was bitterly cold outside. The small hunting blind barely offered enough space for Rachel and her father to sit, uncomfortably perched atop rickety stools. Although Texas was known for its mild weather, occasionally during the winter it would get unreasonably cold. Luckily, Rachel was nestled in her dad's giant, camouflage hunting jacket. Easily three times too big for her eleven-year-old frame, it wrapped her in thick layers of warmth, much like a hug from the jacket's owner. Rachel buried her face in the fabric. It smelled like her dad: like his deodorant and gun cleaner. She was sitting slumped precariously on the unstable hunting stool, trying to keep her eyes open in the cold hazy winter, when she saw the buck amongst the trees. Large and gray, it wandered carefully into the small clearing, approaching the deer feeder suspiciously.

Rachel's heart began to pound wildly. Reaching out with small, cold hands, she gripped the borrowed rifle and raised it carefully. Her father did the same, positioning his own rifle through the small slit in the blind. He could see his daughter's hands nervously fluttering over the rifle. She had practiced for this moment. The rifle was not new to her, he had made sure she knew how to use it before bringing her on this trip.

Nothing could ruin a hunting trip like an inexperienced shot, an injured animal, and a long trek through the wilderness to try to find it and put it out of its misery. Rachel knew how to shoot, and she was good, but this was a different experience. Black and white targets down range had much less consequences than hunting. Her father could tell she was beginning to panic as she balanced the rifle on the wooden frame of the hunting blind and bent next to it, peering through the scope.

Rachel watched the buck through the scope as it continued to root through the grass, munching on corn, occasionally flicking the drizzling rain off its ears. He almost blended in with the forest that surrounded him, gray and devoid of color in the dead of winter, the trees naked and reaching branches toward an overcast, cold sky. Her hands shook as she reached up and flicked off the safety. She was breathing rapidly, as if she had just run miles and miles. The image through the scope shook unsteadily, the world in an earthquake of nerves as the blood in Rachel's ears roared loudly.

Buck fever. Her dad had warned her about this. Even seasoned hunters experienced this panic occasionally. What had her dad said to do?

She had come on this trip because she loved spending time with her dad. When he asked her to go hunting with him, she jumped at the chance. Her older sister wouldn't go, saying that hunting was boring. She much preferred fishing. Stephanie was always going on fishing trips with her dad, so many that Stephen even had a nickname for Stephanie. She was his Fisher Girl.

Rachel, on the other hand, hated fishing. Fish were slimy and smelled terrible, and she always came home empty-handed and sunburned. Stephen didn't take her on those trips anymore because he knew how much she hated them. Even so, Rachel wanted to spend time with her dad and yearned for an activity that could just be theirs, like her sister and fishing.

Rachel did like shooting and had practiced enough that she was pretty good. This trip had been a blast so far. They had bought snacks for the road, and her dad had let her pick the music. She had picked Rush of course, because it was her favorite of her dad's bands. She liked it when he sang along with the songs, even though he was not a good singer by any means. Still, his voice cracking as he tried to hit the high notes of *Temple of Syrinx* was one of her favorite sounds. He never cared what he sounded like. He just loved the music. After a long road trip of good music, laughter, and salty snacks, they had slept in the car at the campground. It had been really late, and they were too exhausted to set anything up. Rachel had wrapped herself tightly in a large purple comforter and had woken with her face pressed against the cold window.

The next morning, they had set up in a hunting blind before the sun even rose but didn't see anything for hours. Eventually, they gave up and had breakfast at a little diner in Leakey which had the largest pancakes Rachel had ever seen. She had sat and listened to her dad talk to a family friend at the breakfast table, soaking in her father's stories and laughter. Now, at the blind the following evening, after waiting and waiting in the biting cold, they finally saw something. And she was going to blow it if she couldn't calm down.

She could feel her father's presence, could sense him looking at her. She knew he could see her shaking. But she wouldn't look at him. She had to remember everything he had taught her. She could do this. She wouldn't let him down.

Breathe, her father would tell her. *Breathe and take your time. Don't panic. You know how to do this. Breathe.*

Stephen watched as his daughter shook. She was going to miss if she didn't calm down. She was panicking as she tried to steady her aim.

She wasn't going to make it. He leaned over his rifle and zeroed in on the deer, ready to clean up a sloppy shot.

Then out of the corner of his eye, he saw her sit up carefully, backing away from the scope. Is she quitting?

Rachel closed her eyes and took a deep breath through her nose, letting the oxygen fill her lungs completely. She released her breath slowly, deliberately, and took a few more calm, steady breaths. Pride filled him, as she slowly stopped shaking, remembering her years of training. After a few moments, she bent back over the scope, her nerves under control. Moments later, the shot fired, cracking loudly through the silent winter.

The buck threw back its head, staring at the sky for a moment, its body rigid. Did she miss? Stephen's finger brushed over the trigger, ready to take down the animal.

Seconds later it fell. A neck shot. A perfect shot. Exactly where he had told her to aim.

"YES!" Stephen screamed loudly, his shout echoing through the forest, nearly louder than the rifle shot.

Rachel sat up away from the rifle and grinned at her dad's exuberance.

"Calm under pressure!" he shouted, clapping her on the back with excitement. "You remembered to breathe! You did it, girl!"

Stephen was so excited that they left that night and drove back to San Antonio. He was so proud of his daughter. He told the story over and over to anyone who would listen.

"She was freaking out," he would say. "Panicking. She had a bad case of buck fever. But then she stopped. She took a deep, deep breath. Then slowly squeezed the trigger. That's my girl! Calm under pressure."

Rachel listened to him and smiled, proud that he was proud of her. Proud to share this story with him. Proud to be his hunting buddy.

Take that, Stephanie.

✳ ✳ ✳

I jumped down before the truck came to a complete stop, my bare feet scraping against the hot blacktop of the highway as I raised my AR-15 and slapped it across the hood of the truck. I braced the rifle against my shoulder, finger on the trigger, eyes peering through the sights and centering the red dot of my EOTech on the driver's door, waiting. I steadied myself, anticipating another spray of bullets, knowing I only had two rounds left to return fire. I took a deep, gulping breath of air, letting the oxygen flow through me, attempting to calm the fury that blazed through my body.

This would be the final stand. Either the killer's or mine. And I was ready.

"Get out of the car, you son-of-a-bitch!" I screamed, the fury bursting forth into a vicious roar.

Silence answered me. I shouted again, commanding that he exit the car, demanding that he lie on the ground, my voice reflecting a courage I wasn't sure I could back up with lead. The adrenaline and fury coursing through my body produced angry shouts and bursts of profanity. I shouted at the silent and still Explorer, my eyes ever-fixed on that red dot down the barrel of my AR-15.

There was no movement. Through the shattered back window, I couldn't even make out the killer's figure. I would have seen if he had escaped. I would have seen if he had exited the vehicle. Where was he?

And where were the police?

Time ceased to exist. It warped and stretched, and froze, trapping me in this never-ending moment. Trapped on the highway, the hot blacktop melding with the calluses of my bare feet, the Texas sun beating down on the back of my neck, the cloudless blue sky offering no respite from the unseasonable heat that caused sweat to drip down my forehead, my hands gripping my gun, finger hovering over the trigger waiting for the answering spray of bullets, waiting for that door to open, or for any movement from within. A never-ending moment, where only two bullets protected me from near certain death. Two bullets, and strength that could only come from God that coursed through me, keeping me on my feet, and preventing my knees from buckling.

I stood, frozen there, certain that this was my life now, certain that this hellish moment would stretch from here until eternity, as fury caused the blood to roar in my ears, my rifle trained on the door, until I heard the warble of a megaphone switching on.

"Driver, get out of the car and put your hands in the air," the slightly distorted, but confident voice commanded.

Until that moment, I was so focused on the Explorer in front of me that I didn't even notice the police car that had pulled up behind me. The voice brought relief, like a bucket of cool water pouring over me. I gasped in a desperate breath as that moment of eternity seemed to shatter with the officer's command.

There was no response from the Explorer. Just unnerving, endless silence.

"Driver, get out of the car and put your hands in the air," the megaphone squawked again, making the voice sound tinny and inhuman.

I was done. It had to be over. Realizing that I still had my AR trained on the vehicle, and not wanting any misunderstandings to occur, I carefully laid my rifle down on the hood of the truck. I raised my hands and took a large step backward.

"Not you!" the officer behind me called loudly.

In a split second, I was back in position, rifle raised, aiming at the driver's door. I stood, this time feeling the commanding and reassuring presence of the police at my back as the officer continued to call out through the megaphone. I wasn't alone now. Now, I was the back up.

I stood my ground, my rifle fixed on the Explorer until I heard the sound of more sirens and saw police cars filled with heavily armed officers crowd the highway. I stood there, tense and waiting until it was abundantly clear I was no longer needed, and until I could see more firearms trained on the still-silent Explorer than I cared to count. Then, and only then did I put my AR-15 down. My legs and hands began to shake as I finally let go of my rifle.

Later, I would learn that I was on scene for about seven minutes before Officer Franklin Ashton arrived. Seven minutes with my rifle trained on the killer's car. Seven minutes expecting to be barraged with bullets.

Seven minutes in hell.

It hadn't felt like seven minutes.

It had felt like a lifetime.

✳ ✳ ✳

There was commotion by the street as the next-door neighbor, Mike Jordan, pulled up in his blue Mustang.

"Pam," he called out, cracking the window.

Pam turned.

"I heard the police talking. There was a crash down 539. I think Stephen is there."

"Is he ok?' Pam responded.

"I don't know. Get in."

Pam opened the passenger door.

"Let me come with you!" Rachel called out, stepping away from the little girl for the moment, following at her heels. "I need to know that he is alright!"

"I will call you!" her mother answered as she closed the door. "Stay here."

The Mustang pulled away with squealing tires. Here. Stay here, where the air smelled of death.

✽ ✽ ✽

Pam was not from Texas. She grew up in St. Louis County, Missouri. In fact, if someone mentioned Texas, she would roll her eyes. All Texans were so arrogant. They were obnoxious, and too proud of their state for their own good.

"I'll never live in Texas," Pam had said in college, after dealing with a particularly annoying Texan in one of her classes.

"Never say never," her mom always told her. "God likes to challenge your nevers."

A few years later, Pam found herself moving to Texas to get away from the cold winters of Missouri and to move closer to her oldest sister and her family. It was ok, though, because surely, she would never marry a Texan.

"Never say never," her mom would remind her. "Because God likes to challenge your nevers."

She first met Stephen at the singles group in church. Pam was shy and reserved. Stephen was loud and talkative. Big groups intimidated Pam. Big groups were Stephen's bread and butter. The first time she saw him, he had a girl under each arm and was standing in a group of friends, his bold laughter filling the room. Pam had rolled her eyes and made a mental note to stay away. Surely, they would never get along. This was one of those Texans she needed to avoid.

Never say never.

Months later, they were close friends. Late night trips to IHOP with Stephen and his roommate, David, were a staple of her week. Pam would sit and listen to Stephen and David tell stories for hours over chili bean and cheese omelets and burned coffee. She had learned to recognize he was friends with everyone he met. The two women under his arms the day she first saw him were just that, friends. After all, Stephen never met a stranger.

For their third date, after he finally asked her out, Stephen picked her up on his motorcycle. She never thought she would ride one of those.

She should have remembered what her mother told her.

As Stephen leaned into curves and the highway rushed by beneath them, Pam was frightened and held onto him so tightly she was sure her hands had left permanent dents in his side. Stephen's passion for things was contagious, however, and Pam soon found herself applying for a motorcycle license. Never in a million years had she thought she would learn to ride a motorcycle.

From the moment Pam met Stephen, life did not go as she expected. She never thought she would marry a Texan, and she married the most obnoxious, proud Texan she could find. She never thought she would end up using her bachelor's degree to teach her three children at home, instead of teaching at a public or private school. She never thought visits to the local shooting range would become a weekly family affair. She never thought she would end up living in a little town in the middle of nowhere, barely even mentioned on most maps. But Pam was happier in her life with Stephen, and more blessed than she had ever thought possible. Before long, as her children grew older, Pam realized that she had become the thing she had feared.

Pam was becoming a Texan.

And she couldn't be happier, in her small town, with her wonderful little family, and proud Texan husband. Because life was wonderful, and full of joy here. Stressful, yes. Inconvenient, sometimes. But overall, Pam was incredibly happy in her small town, with her simple and blessed life.

Besides, bad things never happened here.

***

Pam and Mike did not speak as they sped down 539. Instead, they sat in a tense silence which seemed louder than they could bear. Unspoken grief and confusion filled the air. The familiar road rushed by – green fields, the Cibolo Creek, gnarled trees, the Polley Mansion – all these familiar sights made unfamiliar by the shock which weighed heavily on their hearts.

It seemed forever before they reached the barricade: a single Volunteer Fire Department truck parked across the road. They could see a line of police cars, the small amount of traffic being rerouted, and the swarm of flashing red and blue lights. Mike pulled over on the side of the road, and Pam jumped out of the car, ignoring the directions of the officer who tried to wave at them to turn around. Her eyes strained to see past the cop cars, strained to see the wreck.

She could see a grey Explorer alone in an open field. Police officers were milling about on the highway. About a hundred yards away, there was a pickup truck in the middle of the road. She stepped closer as the volunteer firefighter approached her.

Then she saw him, by the back of a police car, talking with several uniformed officers. He stood, waving both hands above his head, trying to catch her attention. She would have recognized his wild white hair and beard anywhere.

Good God, why was he barefoot?

Only when she saw him waving, unscathed, surrounded by police, did she allow herself to take a deep breath – a breath her body had desperately needed.

Pam, who had not stopped praying since her husband had called her, which seemed an eternity ago, whispered a fervent prayer of thanks to God for keeping him safe.

***

When Stephen decided to ask Pam to marry him, he wanted to make it a grand, romantic affair she would never forget. He loved this quiet girl from Missouri whose quick wit and biting sarcasm had become essential to his day. A woman whose quiet strength ran deeper than he understood, and whose faith was stronger than any he had seen. This was the woman with whom he wanted to spend his life and start a family. He had big plans to sweep her off her feet with romance.

"Should I buy her a ring, or do you think she will want this one?" Stephen had asked his mother, showing her his grandmother's simple, silver wedding ring, with small stones inlaid in the band.

His mother, Pat, was so excited she could barely contain herself. "You know Pam," she had told him. "She isn't a super flashy girl. She's a tomboy and isn't really into all that glitz. I say give her that one, and if she doesn't like it, you can take her to pick one out together."

So, it was settled. With his grandmother's ring in his pocket, Stephen set out with Pam on the grand adventure which he had planned: First stop, was breakfast at his parents' house. Then they'd make the drive to the Texas coast, where Stephen planned to propose on the beach as the sun rose above the waves. It would be beautiful.

This made for a very early breakfast. Pat would be up anyway. Delbert, Stephen's father, was a truck driver, and Pat, the devoted country wife, had been getting up at three in the morning for decades to fix breakfast for him before he left for work. When they arrived that morning, Pam was surprised to find a feast on the breakfast table, the likes of which would please a king. As the couple ate homemade biscuits and gravy, bacon, eggs and sausage, Pat watched with a secret glint in her eyes.

"You didn't cook all this for us, did you?" Pam asked her, feeling slightly guilty for all the work this must have required. "You really shouldn't have gone to all the trouble."

Pat brushed off her comment. "No, honey, I get up and cook breakfast every morning for Delbert. It really was no trouble."

"Every morning?" Pam asked incredulously.

As Pat nodded, Pam turned to Stephen. "If we ever get married," she proclaimed. "Don't you expect this from me!"

Pat had to leave the room to keep from laughing.

Soon enough, they were on their way, barreling through the early morning darkness in Pam's '88 Jeep Wrangler. The highway speeds beat at their faces with cool wind, but they talked as much as they could through the noise on the way down. When they made it across the ferry to Port Aransas, Stephen realized his mistake.

He hadn't thought to check the weather.

They made it to the beach as the sun rose over the waves, but the beach was strewn with trash and crawling with people.

Gilbert, a category five hurricane, had just visited town and wreaked havoc on the beach. Amidst all of Stephen's careful planning, he had completely forgotten about mother nature.

So, the sun rose across the beach, and Stephen kept the ring in his pocket. It wasn't the time. Maybe he would propose at lunch.

Lunch wasn't much better. The diner where they planned to eat was closed for repairs. They ended up getting something cheap, and fast. With not much else to do, they gave up and drove back to San Antonio.

Another thing Stephen forgot: sunscreen. At the beach, and in the jeep with the top and doors removed, the sun had been given ample opportunity to destroy their skin. By the time they returned to San Antonio, they were dehydrated, sunburned, and windblown. Stephen's wiry black hair was an untamable bird's nest, and his skin was bright red and raw. Nevertheless, they were determined to do something today, something to make up for the disappointing trip to the beach.

So, they rented a movie, got take-out, and went back to Stephen's house. They were both too tired to go out anywhere.

Stephen watched Pam, who was curled up on his couch, wrapped in a blanket, her face bright red from the sun, her hair pulled into a tangled ponytail. He had planned the perfect day. He had wanted there to be romance. More than anything though, he wanted to marry this girl.

"Will you marry me?" he blurted out.

Pam glanced down at him. He was on his back on the floor, in his beach clothes, sunburned and windswept. He looked so vulnerable.

She laughed.

"I'm serious," Stephen responded, propping himself up on his elbow, looking confused.

"I know," Pam laughed again.

Years later, when asked by her children how their father had proposed, Pam would smile and sometimes even chuckle slightly.

"It was perfect," she would tell them. "It was perfect, and romantic. I wouldn't change a thing."

✳ ✳ ✳

Finally, Rachel's phone rang.

"He is here," Pam said, the relief clear in her voice. "The killer crashed. DPS won't let me go down there, but I can see him."

Relief washed over her.

"When can we see him?"

"I don't know. Probably not for a while. I'll let you know more when I can."

The next hours passed in a blur. They carried water to victims. They stood helplessly on the sidelines and stared. They comforted those they could. They held each other when they could not.

Eventually, their brother, Blake, and his wife, Heather showed up, along with Bruce, Stephanie's fiancé, their faces pale and grief stricken, their questions unanswerable.

They stayed at the church for a while, trying to help, trying to do good, and busy themselves against the fear and overwhelming confusion they all felt.

Rachel helped Kathleen rinse the blood from the little girl's hair and find her a change of clothes. Stephanie gave her statement to a stricken sheriff's deputy as Bruce rubbed her back comfortingly. Matt stood restlessly, not knowing where to go, standing in the shadow of the house with a wordless Heather and Blake.

After a while, a man stumbled across the street. He was streaked in blood, his gray dress pants and sky-blue button-up shirt wrinkled and grimy.

A Town Called Sutherland Springs

Kevin, one of the many neighbors surrounding the church, helped him to a seat and handed him water pilfered from his own kitchen.

Kathleen went over to check on him. After a few questions, she asked him if he knew the little girl.

The shock on his face cleared away for a moment as he nodded. She was his stepdaughter. When she saw him, no words were spoken, no tears shed. He simply pulled her into his lap, and they held each other in wordless sorrow, clinging to one another as if their very lives depended on it. In that moment, as the two family members embraced, taking comfort in each other's presence and each other's survival, the world seemed to stop. It was just the two of them. The two of them had made it through unspeakable horror.

And for now, that was enough.

✣ ✣ ✣

John Holcombe first met Crystal at Oak Hills Animal Hospital. They were both single at the time. The receptionist at the front desk hinted they should get together, but they both shrugged off her comments. Neither were interested.

Years passed, and John ran into Crystal again. She joined First Baptist Church of Sutherland Springs with her husband, Pete, and five beautiful children: Phillip, Gregory, Emily, Megan, and Evelyn. Tragically, Pete's life was cut short by heart problems, and he passed away, leaving his family behind.

Crystal and her kids were left reeling and trying to pick up the pieces. John didn't intend to take up a family. He wasn't prepared to have a wife and children, but he could clearly see the effect that Pete's death had on the kids, especially the boys. The boys were in John's Sunday school class, and it broke his heart to see them hurting. So, John invited the family to join him at GattiLand for arcade games and pizza. They had fun running wildly through the restaurant in the flashing lights of the arcade games, filling the machines with quarters, getting tickets for prizes, and eating greasy pizza. That is how it started. A few weeks later, Crystal invited John to the movies with her family. They went to the Arcadia, a little three-screen theater in Floresville. John doesn't even remember what movie they saw – he just remembers feeling honored to be included. His presence had a positive effect on the kids as well, since they craved a male presence in their lives.

Shortly afterward, Crystal asked John to sit with her family in church. Crystal was young, attractive, and vibrant. Her exuberant light drew people to her like moths. Because of this, she was getting a lot of unwanted attention from the single men in the community. John joined her in church to act as a buffer to these men and shield her from their advances. That's all it was intended to be at first. Just a friend helping another friend. Little did John know at the time that Crystal's light was reaching the dark corners of his heart which had hardened itself to love.

Soon afterward, John was joining family events, seamlessly fitting into shish-kabob dinners by the pond, watching the sun sparkling off the water as the kids played outside. They spent time together at church, and John taught the kids in Sunday school. Slowly but surely, Crystal and her kids became an integral part of John's daily life.

On December 15th, 2011, he found himself proposing to Crystal in her living room. He hadn't expected to start his life as a husband with five children, but these weren't just regular kids. They were the most remarkable kids John had ever met, and they had already stolen his heart and planted themselves there. At least, the part that didn't already belong to Crystal.

They were married on Easter Sunday, April 8th, 2012. They didn't make a big fuss of it or send out invitations. They simply got married in a small ceremony after church service, at the church they both loved. In this way, John went from a single man, living alone, to a family man with a wife and five wonderful children. This was never his plan. But John learned God's plans were so much bigger and more wonderful than he could understand.

Crystal was a fantastic, godly wife and mother. She was full of the Holy Spirit, and shone with a beautiful grace and compassion, and an inward and outward beauty, the likes of which John had never seen. She was quick to forgive and quick to love. She was the very embodiment of the godly wife laid out in Proverbs 31.

Crystal's hands were blessed with a healing talent which could only come from God. She cured everything she touched- whether it was a dying plant, a sick animal, a crying child, or a weary husband. She had unbelievable patience and a nurturing love for the hurting.

This was on full display when a small, dying kitten showed up at their house one summer. The creature had six toes on each foot and a crooked, broken tail. It had diarrhea and was crusty and missing patches of fur. On top of the mange, the poor kitten had ringworm. Though some may have been repulsed by the sick kitten, Crystal responded with love. She brought the kitten into their home, and patiently nursed it back to health. She named it "Baby Kitty" and treated it with as much love and affection as she poured into everyone around her. She didn't care that playing with it and snuggling it spread a bout of ringworm through her entire household- the little animal needed love, and Crystal had plenty of love to offer.

Crystal made the best tea the world had to offer. She had a knack for understanding the best things to put in a cup to make it flavorful and delicious, with just a dash of sugar for sweetness. She would spend time concocting medicine out of oils and other ingredients which could cure a staph infection or a bad earache. She spent hours poring over the curriculum with which to homeschool her five children, searching for the perfect one, and ingrained the love of Christ and Godly principles in their attitudes and actions. She led by example. It was impossible to know Crystal and not see the light of the Holy Spirit shining through her- especially in her bright and beautiful smile. Her intense love for everyone she met was one of the biggest parts of Crystal's legacy. It changed people and the world for the better.

Crystal enjoyed going to the beach, volunteering at church, and playing games. She loved to go shopping with her husband and had an orange belt in Karate.

A Town Called Sutherland Springs

Gregory Lynn Hill had just turned thirteen. Greg, who hated to be called Gregory- was far from an angsty teenager, though. The boy avoided fights and would willingly surrender any of his belongings if someone else was in need. He was a peacekeeper and had the loving spirit of his mother. It was rare to see him without a jolly smile which spread throughout his entire body.

He loved to help people, whether it was helping his mother with dinner (where Greg developed his own knack for cooking) or helping his sisters practice karate outside (he himself was a green belt). Greg was a dependable and joyful boy.

Greg loved Star Wars, video games, and movies. He had recently received a Nintendo Switch and would dive into the world of Mario or Hyrule, spending quality time chasing down opponents in go-karts, throwing turtle shells, or attempting to liberate Princess Zelda. These passions fed Greg's bright and vivid imagination. It was not unusual to peer through the windows of the house to see him outside, swinging a stick or a broom as if it was a mighty sword or lightsaber- steeped in some imaginary battle which raged on in his creative mind. It was this creativity that drove Greg to join a 4-H Robotics team, which ignited a passion for technology and robotics that he planned to utilize in his future.

Greg was always incredibly grateful and insightful, and had a strong faith in Jesus Christ. He loved going to church with his family and shone with the love of the Lord. He very much resembled his father- Peter Hill- in both appearance and behavior.

Emily Rose Hill was eleven years old. She was responsible beyond her years, and very obedient. She lived to serve others and was constantly searching for something which needed to be done. She was fiercely independent and motivated, and as the oldest daughter in the family had taken on a nurturing, motherly attitude towards her two younger sisters. She loved to help them get ready in the morning and spent ample time brushing their hair and helping them get dressed. She could be counted on to take care of her siblings, as well as her rabbit, and Batman- her pet cat- without being asked. Emily was not satisfied unless she was able to make everyone's life a little bit easier.

Stormy, a member of First Baptist Church, had been teaching Emily how to perform magic. She loved magic and picked up the tricks fairly quickly. Often, she would gather her family in the living room and put on a magic show, impressing everyone with how efficiently she was learning new tricks. Although Emily was initially shy, she did not have a problem performing in front of others and had recently begun to break out of her shell. She had a beautiful singing voice and was looking forward to joining the church choir one day. Her voice was clear and angelic, and brought peace to those who heard it.

Emily loved to cook and competed in 4-H County Food Show and Food Challenge, where she had recently won third place for the most delicious quesadillas. She also competed in 4-H Archery and was a very good shot. Like the rest of her family, Emily loved karate. She was a purple belt, and loved to teach her moves to John when he returned home from work.

A Town Called Sutherland Springs

Emily was a passionate, loving girl whose love for God was evident in her treatment of everyone she met.

Megan Gail Hill was nine and completely, utterly adorable. Her attitude, personality, and appearance were overwhelmingly charming, earning her the nickname "Mega-Cuteness" from Grumpy, John's father. Megan was loving and exuberant, with an intense passion for her family. When John would return from work, she would run through the house and fly into his arms. Megan and the youngest, Evelyn, would often playfully fight over who got the first hug or the first kiss, and who loved him the most. Megan always let her family know how much she loved them.

Like her mother, Megan had a way with animals. Once, over at her grandparents' house, Megan spotted a wild, feral cat which wandered the property. Even though she was warned that the creature would not let anyone touch it, Megan grabbed a pillow and wrapped the cat up so its claws could not reach her. Within minutes, the animal had formed a deep bond with Megan and was no longer a wild, untouchable mess of claws and hissing. She named him Prr Prr, pronounced Purr Purr, after the contented noise the cat made whenever it spotted her.

Megan was very playful and creative, and loved to draw. Once, she created a Pass Card for John, which he was required to carry in his wallet. The card was skillfully made, and fun, so he carried it with honor. Randomly, as John was going about his day at home, Megan would materialize in front of him and demand to see his pass card. Before he could get by, John would have to produce the card from his wallet, which she would then validate before returning it to him and letting him pass.

Like her sister, Megan was enrolled in Archery and Food Challenge in 4-H. And like the rest of the family, Megan was taking karate at the American Blackbelt Institute in Floresville and had received a Gold Belt. Her playful spirit and loving compassion very much resembled her mother's.

In July 2017, Crystal became pregnant with what would be her sixth child. John and Crystal weren't really planning on having a baby at the time- their family was already big, and they were very busy. So, when she discovered she was pregnant, she was initially nervous to tell John, unsure exactly how he would react. There was no reason for her to be nervous. If the last few years had taught John anything, it was that God sometimes ignored his plans and substituted them with His own. John had learned to trust in Him. So, when she finally told him, he was surprised, and both were elated.

The news gave them a joyful purpose to work toward. Together, they ramped up their remodeling plans which had been a long-term project. They shopped for maternity clothes, and planned names. Finally, they landed on two names: Carlyn Brite for a girl, and Carlin Dennys for a boy. Carlin meant Champion and resembled Karla, Carolyn, and Charles, who were various relatives that Crystal hoped to honor. Regardless of these official names, the kids in the family referred to the child as Billy Bob. The kids were thrilled when they discovered their mom was pregnant and had already formed a relationship with the baby. They would lean against their mother's belly and speak to their growing sibling, telling the baby how much they already loved their little Billy Bob. Carlin "Billy Bob" Brite Holcombe was due on April 14th, 2018. On November 5th, Crystal was only 18 weeks pregnant, so John hadn't learned if the child was a girl or a boy. He will know when they meet again. Although the child joined their family in Heaven before making an entrance into the world, Carlin Brite had already been wrapped in more love and prayers than most.

Crystal, Greg, Emily, Megan, and Carlin joined the Heavenly chorus on November 5th. John knows they are rejoicing together, with their Grumpy, and Mor Mor, and their biological father, Peter Hill. He knows Emily has added her beautiful and clear voice with the angels, where she will worship God for eternity, and that Crystal can now cradle little Carlin Brite in her arms.

Although John stumbled into the role of husband and father accidentally, he feels blessed beyond measure for the time he spent with his wife and children and knows he will see them again.

Crystal Holcombe and her children were members of the First Baptist Church of Sutherland Springs for eleven years.

Chapter Eight:
A Remnant

Pastor Frank Pomeroy was in Oklahoma, attending a black powder rifle seminar, when he received a text from John Holcombe. He glanced at his phone absently.

Shooting at church.

Frank's brow furrowed.

Surely, you're joking, he responded.

He stared anxiously at his phone, waiting.

No, was the one-word response.

Frank leapt to his feet and walked outside, his face flushed and his blood roaring as he stumbled out into the bright, Oklahoma sun. He began to call everyone he knew at the church. The phone rang and rang as person after person did not respond. He paced quickly, ringing his hands, his mouth dry.

There couldn't have been a shooting. Not in his church. People carried firearms in his church. They were in the country. Surely, someone had a gun. It couldn't be possible. The church was his family, and his 14-year-old daughter was there. But the more numbers he tried, the more Frank was filled with trepidation.

Finally, someone answered.

"What happened?" Frank burst out, as soon as he heard Rod Green's rough voice on the line. "John said there was a shooting, and I can't get a hold of anyone!"

"A shooting?" Rod exclaimed, his voice thick with surprise. "I'm not there, I was going to run an errand."

Frank knew Rod always carried his gun with him. Was anyone else carrying in the church?

"I'm on my way over there now. I'm about ten minutes away."

"Let me know what you find out," Frank responded. "I'm on my way home."

Frank hung up the phone and leapt into his car. He peeled out of the parking lot and began to rush home. The car wasn't moving fast enough. The road seemed to stretch out into eternity as the landscape appeared to crawl by. Frank cried fervent prayers to God as he drove, his hands gripping the steering wheel so tightly that he thought he would pull it from its axis.

Finally, about ten minutes later, his phone rang again. He picked up the phone, with dread rising and suffocating the air all around him.

"What happened?"

Rod's voice was thick with grief so tangible it was like a knife to Frank's heart. "It's bad, Frank. It's real bad."

"Rod, what about Belle?"

The line was quiet for a moment, so quiet that Frank felt as if that terrible silence filled the entire earth. He felt as if he was drowning in it.

"She didn't make it," Rod responded.

It took everything in him not to drop the phone.

✶ ✶ ✶

Pastor Frank Pomeroy and his wife Sherri had never really considered adopting. They already had a handful of biological kids in various stages of adolescence by the time Frank met a little girl who was crying in the sanctuary.

It happened during Vacation Bible School. Groups of small children were roaming through the church, transitioning from classroom to classroom, activity to activity. Frank entered the sanctuary between lessons and heard a little girl crying.

She was up at the altar, a small mess of tears and deep, broken breaths. Frank approached her quickly, his heart breaking at the pitiful sound. When he drew closer and asked what was wrong, the little girl threw herself into his arms.

"My mommy gave me up today," she wailed. "She said she wanted to party and drink more than she wanted me!"

For a long moment, Frank did not know what to say. The little girl's sorrow seized his heart.

Meanwhile, in the nursery, his wife Sherri cradled an 18-month-old baby. She was up for adoption today. As Sherri held the little girl, she knew she was supposed to be her mother.

A Town Called Sutherland Springs

Frank exited the sanctuary at the same time Sherri left the nursery. They locked eyes across the long concrete porch of the church, Frank with a little girl clinging to his large hand and Sherri cradling a precious baby in her arms. They met in the middle, the hot Texas sun casting bright yellow light across the concrete.

"This little girl has fetal alcohol syndrome. She is up for adoption today," Sherri told Frank, her hands holding tight to her precious cargo.

"That's my sister," said Marina, the little girl clinging to Frank.

Frank looked down at the child for a moment, and then back up at his wife. Both knew they were going to adopt these little girls, before they even said anything to each other.

Months later, after going through classes and court sessions, and finding the baby's father so he could sign away his parental rights, Annabelle and Marina were official Pomeroys.

Because of Annabelle's fetal alcohol syndrome, and the bad shape she was in when they adopted her into their family, doctors told Frank and Sherri that it was likely Annabelle would never walk or talk. But they did not know Annabelle. She fought through the pain, the shaking limbs, the difficulty speaking. She would not be defeated. Annabelle went on to exceed everyone's expectations. Though she wasn't necessarily an athlete, she was stronger than everyone told her she would be. Though it was a long, tough battle, Annabelle Pomeroy blossomed with Frank and Sherri as her loving, dedicated parents.

Annabelle- or Belle, as her family often called her- loved the water. She was a natural mermaid, and loved any activity that took her into a pool, river, or lake. She was also definitely a daddy's girl. One of her favorite activities was kayaking with her dad.

The first time Frank put her in a kayak, he waded the boat into the water and prepared for a long lesson teaching her how to paddle and steer. The lesson was not needed. Annabelle was a natural. She was paddling in circles around him before Frank could show her how. He was amazed and a little disconcerted at how quickly she picked it up.

Frank and Annabelle loved to kayak together. They lived right on the Guadalupe River and would travel upriver to Lake Placid and back, which would take about an hour and a half. It was one of Annabelle's favorite things to do.

Once, Frank and Annabelle dragged their kayaks to Canyon Lake. Together, they made the hour-long journey across the sparkling water, to the other bank. There, they skipped rocks, splashed in the water, and talked for a long time. What Frank didn't know was that a storm was blowing in. When he saw the sky start to darken, he rushed Annabelle to the kayaks and panic started to set in. As they began to journey across the lake, the wind picked up, raising the water in waves which grew and grew. As their kayaks crested the waves and then slapped back down onto the lake, Frank would turn to his brave, trusting daughter.

"What is the one rule, Annabelle?" he asked her, over and over again.

"Number one rule!" she called back, maneuvering the bow of her kayak to the back of her father's over and over again. "Don't panic!"

They repeated this, as Frank did his best to maintain a confident exterior. Inside, he was worried. What if her kayak flipped? Would he be able to reach her? Would it matter that she was wearing a life jacket?

Meanwhile, Annabelle paddled, following the lead of her father. She trusted and loved him completely. She was calmer than Frank. She knew her father would take care of her.

Annabelle loved deeply. It did not take much for a person to earn one of her tackle hugs. When she saw someone she loved, and there were many, she would call their name and run across the church. Annabelle would then wrap the person in a one-of-a-kind hug- the kind of wonderful, loving hug which only Annabelle could give. She always found the good side of everyone, even when others couldn't, and trusted people easily. Everyone who knew her knew she was the absolute epitome of joy.

In 2017, Belle transferred to Seguin school district. In Seguin, she had blossomed. She made friends quickly, received good grades, and even landed a part in the school's Christmas play: a production of Elf. In the short time Belle attended Seguin middle school, she became known for her constant smiles and deep-rooted faith. During school reading times, she always took out her Bible and was never afraid to talk to her classmates about the overwhelming love of Jesus.

Annabelle, who loved her family, her church, her animals, and the color purple, is now snuggly held in the arms of her Creator. She had been a member of the First Baptist Church of Sutherlands Springs for 12 years.

※ ※ ※

Alice Garcia stood among the crowd of people who had gathered at the church in Sutherland Springs. EMS darted everywhere and police officers approached the onlookers, taking statements and jotting them down on paper. Alice had been standing there for a while now, in shock. She wanted to do something but didn't know what. When she heard the news, she had been at church in La Vernia. For a while, she didn't believe it. It wasn't until she arrived at the scene that the magnitude of the news sank in. She almost couldn't believe her eyes as EMS hauled the survivors out of the building, holding bloodied gauze and towels to bleeding gunshot wounds, strapping them to stretchers, and sending them off to waiting AirLIFE helicopters. Overhead, helicopters circled, waiting for their chance to land.

Alice approached two women who stood in a daze on the porch of the house across the street.

"What happened?" she asked breathlessly.

"There was a shooting," one replied, her voice hollow and distant, her eyes shocked.

The words had finally sunk into Alice's denial.

So, she stood with the group of onlookers, wringing her hands, and whispering wordless prayers. She wasn't sure what to ask for, so she just pleaded with God to be present. She watched as the Sheriff of Wilson County exited the doors of the church. He looked stricken, and pale. This was, after all, a situation which no one should ever have to witness.

Martha Buford, a local Pastor's wife, began walking through the small clusters of people.

"If you're looking for news about family, go to the community center. We are gathering there. We need to get everyone away."

Martha's words penetrated the fog in Alice's mind. She was in charge of the community center. She was the one with the key.

Alice had lived in Sutherland Springs all her life. So, when someone from the Sutherland Springs Community Association approached her about being president of the Community Center she didn't hesitate. She loved her town. She became president in 2011. Her responsibilities included managing and renting out the community building and handling the scheduling, lights, and use of the baseball field.

"It's locked," Alice told Martha as the crowd began to thin out and head down the street in the direction of the community building. "I should go home and get the keys."

Despite her words, Martha and Alice followed the crowd of crying, desperate people down the road toward the old community building in the heart of town. She should really go home and get the keys. No one would be able to get in. For some reason, although she knew the building was locked, Alice's legs carried her forward.

A small crowd had already gathered. Family members and concerned neighbors clustered around the building, weeping, praying, and holding each other.

"It's locked," someone called out as they approached. "We need the keys."

Alice knew she needed to get them but approached the door anyway. She went to check, even though others had already rattled the old doorknob and pushed against it. This had to be an effect of her shock.

The door to the community building had been hard to open for some time now. The foundations were beginning to shift, and the old, crooked door frame had to be forced open with one's shoulder. And the key, of course.

Alice ascended the ramp, up to the entryway of the building, her shaking hand reaching out to touch the doorknob. As soon as her fingers touched the metal, the door swung open with ease. Alice took a deep breath, staring down the darkened room of the building.

At that moment, Alice knew her life would never be the same again.

* * *

Blake and Heather, Rachel and Matt, and Stephanie and Bruce sat in silence in the living room of the Willeford household. No words passed between them. Nothing anyone could say could explain what had happened, or the grief they all felt. The room was heavy and bleak. The flash of police lights could still be seen through the heavily curtained windows. It was haunting.

Tears had dried on their cheeks. They felt hollow and empty as they sat, afraid to turn on the television. Afraid to hear how many community members had been slaughtered.

A Town Called Sutherland Springs

How did this happen here? Here, in such a small town where everyone knew everyone, and where people seldom even locked their doors at night? A small town whose beating heart was its Baptist Church, which served as an ever-reliable hub of activity, events, festivals, and tent revivals. A church whose congregation never met a stranger, whose doors were always open, and who always offered blessings and praises to God for his goodness. How did this happen here, at home, where they had always felt safe?

How could they feel safe now?

Eventually, the shutting of a car door broke their reverie. Rachel bolted from her chair and ripped the door open. Stephen was stepping onto the porch, shoulders drooping, head down, with Pam at his heels looking equally defeated.

Only when Rachel saw him did she feel like she could breathe again. Only when she saw him did the pulsing knot in her stomach start to unwind.

"Daddy," she cried, wrapping her arms around him, and burying her face in his shoulder.

Together, still clinging to each other, they stepped into the house and closed the door behind them. The rest of the family joined, wrapping arms around each other as if they could keep each other from shattering.

"You are ok," Rachel murmured. "Tell me you are ok."

Stephen spoke for the first time, then, tears pooled in his eyes. "I killed a man, baby," he responded, devastation thick in his voice. "I killed him, but I didn't know what else to do."

You did the right thing.

You saved lives.

You did what you had to do.

Though all true statements, nothing seemed to lessen the weight which was visibly crushing him.

So, instead, they clung to each other and prayed with each other, hoping that this was all just a terrible nightmare.

* * *

The next hours at the community center passed in a frenzy. People arrived desperate for news. Pastors from all over the surrounding area showed up to huddle against the wall, shell shocked and silent. Mourners wept and clung to each other. Their grief was so audible, it could be heard outside the building and down the street. No one knew anything. Names of the survivors and deceased alike were not being released. So, the community clustered together, inside the building, waiting for any scrap of news. Alice milled about, handing out water to people, holding the mourners and praying for them. Her sisters helped prepare food in the kitchen.

Eventually, the Red Cross arrived and cleared the community building of anyone who wasn't family or a spiritual leader. Alice refused to leave. The community building was her responsibility. She would stay and help. So, she began taking names of the family members who were present and fashioned makeshift wrist bands for them out of first aid bandages. She held the hands of the weeping, coaxing them to eat and drink.

A Town Called Sutherland Springs

One man heard the mourners from down the road. His name was Mike Gonzales. He was retired military and had lived in a nearby town for quite some time. Upon learning of the shooting, Mike made his way to the community center. When he saw the people crying, and watched the Red Cross rushing about, Mike knew something needed to be done.

"We need to have a prayer vigil," Mike told the group of pastors, who stood around and stared with wide eyes, untouched cups of steaming coffee gripped in their hands.

"It's too soon," they told him. "We need to wait."

Mike would not wait. "No, we need a memorial. Tonight. We need a prayer vigil. This community needs it."

Everyone shrugged off his words. So, Mike took it upon himself to make it happen. Amidst the chaos, he went out and found a PA system. He and his family personally bought candles and spread the word.

That night, hundreds gathered at the post office across the street from the church. Neighbors, families, residents of the surrounding towns, and even Governor Greg Abbott arrived. The people gathered close together and prayed, the light of the candles shining on tear-stained faces. Worship songs played over the PA system which Mike had set up. The watching crowd lifted hands and voices, their shared grief making the weight a little bit lighter for everyone present.

Police officers, homeland security, FBI, and Texas Rangers continued sifting through the crime scene into the late hours of the night. The faithful voices of the community rose up all around them, lending strength to their exhausted hearts.

Stephen Willeford & Rachel Howe

✷ ✷ ✷

The day after was full of emotions for Frank Pomeroy. He had driven home as fast as he was able. His wife, Sherri, who was in Florida helping with disaster relief, had found a flight home. One of the hardest things Frank ever had to do was tell his wife the news over the phone. Now, they were here, at their church. They could hardly tell it was their church. There was yellow crime scene tape, tall metal fencing, and huge tents surrounding the building. Agents of all kinds- FBI, Texas Rangers, Police officers, and Homeland Security surrounded the property. All of them wanted a statement from Frank and Sherri, who did their best to answer their questions through their shock. They had even had to help identify one of the congregants when the medical staff and officers could not.

Now they stood in the trodden grass in front of the church, waiting for the officers to take them down the road, where a giant swarm of press waited behind barricades with cameras and microphones, hungry and greedy for another piece of news. Frank and Sherri clung to each other, grief like a heavy fog clouding their minds and numbing them down to their bones. Frank looked toward the barricade, wanting to get this over with, wanting this day to end.

A man parted from the thick group of reporters. He passed the barricades and passed the officers guarding them. The man was one of the tallest people Frank had ever seen. Easily close to seven feet tall, he was not exactly inconspicuous, and yet he walked down the road, in the open, as if unseen by all the officers and agents around him. He was impeccably dressed in a full suit, tie, and shining black shoes which didn't seem to have a speck of dirt on them. His skin was the darkest that Frank had ever seen – as black as the darkest night. His dark eyes were fixed on Frank and Sherri as he walked through the groups of officers, past the crime scene tape, and onto the grass in front of the church. He approached them stoically.

"God sent me here," he told them. "I would like to pray for you."

The giant man placed his hands on their shoulders and began to pray. Most of what he said, Frank could not remember. The cloud of grief which swirled in his mind took away the meaning of most of the words he heard. When the officers came to take Frank and Sherri to the press conference, the man walked with them.

"Don't forget to give all the glory to God," the man told Frank. "Don't forget to keep the focus on Him."

With the man's words ringing in their ears, Frank and Sherri approached the throng of cameras, lights, and microphones. They stepped past the barrier and up to the podium as the officer introduced them to the media. Sherri's heart ached, but she kept her mind focused on the words of the stranger. Keep God in the center. Keep the focus on Him. Sherri told the media that the focus should not just be on the loss of their daughter's life, but on the entire family that they had lost. She begged the media not to forget Sutherland Springs, as their town lay in ruin. And she praised God for the knowledge that her daughter was not alone in the church, but was surrounded by family.

After their statement, Frank and Sherri had begun to back away when a persistent reporter shouted out a question.

"What do you make of what happened?" he asked, eager for a story as the couple tried to extract themselves from the crowd.

"I don't understand," Frank responded. "But I know my God does. And that's where I'll leave that."

As they backed away, Frank searched the crowd for the man who had prayed with him. He had completely vanished.

✳ ✳ ✳

For a long time, Frank and Sherri did not know who the tall, dark man was, or from whence he came. He entered their lives out of nowhere, at exactly the time when they needed him, and had urged them to remember God. With their thoughts scattered across the ruined building of their church, the reminder was desperately needed. For a while, Frank was sure he was an angel.

A few months later, Sherri found him online. He was a pastor from New York. How he arrived so quickly, all the way across America, only a day after the shooting, or why he was in their town at all remained a mystery to them. The man never reached out to them again. He came all the way from New York to encourage them for five minutes, pray with them, and tell them exactly what they needed to hear.

Frank is still not quite convinced he wasn't an angel.

✳ ✳ ✳

A Town Called Sutherland Springs

Frank walked back down the road as the press continued shouting questions. He felt destroyed, shattered. He did not question God's goodness, or mercy, but did not know how to move forward from here. He only knew one thing: he had to go see the survivors in the hospital. As he approached the sanctuary, he spotted Mark Collins. Mark used to be his associate pastor, and now led his own church in Yorktown. He knew the people who had died as well as Frank did and had arrived to help the survivors and the Pomeroys in any way he could.

"I'm done," Frank told him, his voice as raw as an open wound. "I've got to go see my people."

"I'll take you," Mark said, leading Frank to his vehicle.

Frank wanted to drive himself, but Mark refused to let him. Mark rightly recognized that Frank was not in an emotional state to drive safely. Though Frank knew he was right, it still made him mad.

His church was gone. He was done. His soul felt completely depleted, raw, and empty. With most of his congregation either gone or in the hospital, and their building in complete ruin, Frank was sure the First Baptist Church of Sutherland Springs was gone forever. He just knew he had to go see his people, the remainder of his family, and try to understand what was left of his life here. The hour-long drive to San Antonio passed in a grief-tinged, tense silence. The whole time, Frank didn't question God's presence, but did not see sense in any of this madness. He did not understand what the plan was and prayed desperately.

When Mark finally pulled into the parking lot of the first hospital, Frank steeled himself for the conversations and the grief that lay ahead. He opened the door, ready to encourage his congregation, pray with them, and assure them that somehow God had a plan in all of this.

✶ ✶ ✶

Frank Pomeroy received his Pastor's license in 2001. At the time, he was working with a church in La Vernia, Texas, as a Youth Pastor. He never really intended to preach full time but planned on jumping around and filling in when needed. Then, two jobs presented themselves. One was in a small town outside of Stockdale – the other was in Sutherland Springs.

When Frank interviewed in Sutherland Springs, he learned how small the church was. Just five families. They couldn't afford a full-time pastor and had just experienced a fracture in their church body. The small church had shrunk to a measly size and was experiencing problems Frank wasn't sure he was qualified to take on. The other town offered him more benefits. It would be less of a struggle. Frank discussed plans with his wife, and they both agreed he should pass on Sutherland Springs. The decision wasn't sitting quite right with Frank, though. So, as he was pulling his car into the driveway, Frank thought of Gideon and the wool he laid on the ground to test God's plan.

Alright, God, he prayed. *I'm going to lay out my wool. I am going to call and accept the position in Elm Creek unless you tell me differently, right now.*

A Town Called Sutherland Springs

No more than five seconds later, Frank's phone rang. It was Ted Montgomery, from Sutherland Springs.

"Hey, Pastor!" Ted exclaimed when he answered the phone. "The weirdest thing just happened. I was walking through the VA hospital, and your card slipped out of my Bible. I don't know why, but I felt like God was telling me to call you and let you know that we still really hope you decide to come lead our church. Have you thought any more about your decision?"

Flabbergasted, Frank responded that he was working out an answer, and he would let him know. After a brief conversation, Frank hung up the phone. He stared out his windshield in momentary shock, before calling his wife.

"Well, God told me which church I need to preach at," he told her when he heard her voice on the other line.

"Oh no," Sherri responded, already knowing what he was going to say.

Since then, Frank and Sherri have been leading the First Baptist Church of Sutherland Springs. With God's guidance and the help of the beautiful people who attended, the church had grown and become a close-knit family. It was now a real presence in the town of Sutherland Springs. Frank and Sherri were so glad God chose this small, country church which could barely afford to pay them every week and whose building was falling apart, but whose congregants proved themselves to be faithful and steadfast.

* * *

Frank exited San Antonio Military Medical Center into the cold November night. It was past eleven. He had spent hours in the hospital rooms of the survivors, talking with them and hearing their stories. What he heard there changed him.

Each person was praising God. They told Frank how excited they were to get out of the hospital and go back to church. They told him how great God was, and how blessed they were to have a powerful testimony. They were joyful that they had been chosen to tell the world about the Lord.

Frank had entered the hospital feeling like a dishrag which had been squeezed and wrung until the threads were bare. He had expected nonetheless to encourage the people in their hospital rooms, to pour his heart and soul into them, and to be strong for them. But he left the hospital full of growing hope. It was his congregants who ignited that hope in his heart. If they could be so strong in the face of that unspeakable evil and the horrendous things they witnessed, how could he not?

The sky was clear. Overhead, thousands of stars shone down on him. In the trees outside the hospital, grackles sang in chorus. As Frank looked up, the cold air stinging his face, the words of God in the book of Job rang in his mind.

Where were you when I laid the foundations of the earth?

In that moment, Frank felt as if his mind cleared like a defroster on the windshield of a car, clearing away every speck of fog and ice. He heard the birds and saw the bright, shining stars. He knew that, come hell or high water, his people would be stronger, and God's church would stand taller.

"We have a remnant," he told Mark, the broken pieces of his heart beginning to knit back together with the strength of the Lord pouring into him. "We are going to make it through this."

Frank had no idea how to move forward, but for the first time since he got that text message, he knew there was a future for his church. Their story was only beginning. He only had to trust God, minute by minute, and He would show him the path forward. They were going to win this fight. Satan had lashed out strongly against his community, but he would not be victorious. The Holy Spirit was present in every single hospital room, shining through the eyes and words of those who survived.

And Frank knew, as he always had, that God was moving in Sutherland Springs

✲ ✲ ✲

For my family, the following days ran together- a blur of police cars, news trucks, and swarming reporters crawling over the scene like greedy ants, planting themselves in the yards of the victims and survivors. Their microphones were inescapable, their patronizing understanding of our community's pain barely masking their delight at an inside scoop. Reporters harassed mourners at memorials and snapped pictures of families walking to the candlelight vigil, of families praying, weeping, and trying to piece together a private moment to mend their shattered hearts. They trapped me and my family in our home like it was a prison. I couldn't talk to them. Not yet. I had barely had a moment to process what had happened and was in no shape to be on national news.

The police did what they could. They put crime scene tape up around our house and warned reporters to stay off private property, but that didn't stop the most eager. They still came and knocked on our doors, delivering bribes of fruit baskets, muffins, and an endless barrage of business cards.

We want to hear your story.

We want to know more about the hero.

We will tell the world what you want them to hear.

All the promises felt like lies as the media already began pushing gun control as a solution, all the while ignoring the fact that the rifle they demonized was the very rifle I used to stop the murderer's killing spree.

Well, Stephen is a responsible gun owner, they said.

He is trained.

He is different from the rest.

He had his gun unloaded in a safe, and that's what we like to see.

Some outlets even reported that what I did was inconsequential. The murderer was already leaving the church, they claimed. So, an AR-15 definitely did not stop the slaughter.

Meanwhile, I tortured myself. How many lives could have been saved, I wondered, if my gun had been loaded? If I could have saved time by not having to unlock the safe? If I had had quicker access, saving precious seconds. Every shot I heard as I entered the combination of the safe and loaded my gun was like a punch in my gut.

If only I had gotten there sooner, I told myself. If only I had saved more people.

If only...

These nightmares kept me and my family up at night. When we closed our eyes, we still saw the blood. Heard the gunshots. When my family slept, they still waited anxiously for news of me. Where was their father? Was he alive?

Friends came and went. They brought food, prayers, and condolences. They gathered around us, protecting us from the cameras and the pestering questions from reporters. They held us as we wept. They helped keep us strong.

Days passed. I gave a few interviews to outlets I trusted to treat the story fairly. Then, I grew tired of telling the same story. I grew tired of the word, "hero".

After all, I was a survivor too. The actions of the killer had shaken the very foundations of my life as well. I was not just some badass who took out the boogie man. Secretly, I did not feel like a badass at all, or a hero. I felt shattered, my very being altered.

I just wanted to feel like myself again.

This is your new normal, they told me.

You may not ever feel like yourself again.

You have to find a way to process this into your daily life.

Your new normal.

But how could this ever feel normal?

Chapter Nine: Finding Hope

A week later, Alice brought a car full of donated flowers to River Oaks Baptist Church. River Oaks was down 539 from Sutherland Springs and was led by Paul and Martha Buford. They had volunteered their building as a headquarters for grieving family members and counselors. Dozens of emotional support dogs were brought in to cuddle and comfort the hurting, and pastors and grief counselors from all over had made the church their semi-permanent residence.

Alice hadn't stopped moving and working all week. But now, as she entered the River Oaks chapel, her arms loaded with donated bouquets of flowers, all the energy drained from her. She sat heavily on the couch in the foyer, the grief from the week welling up inside her and taking away her ability to walk. Alice began to cry, the flowers clutched tightly in her hands, her tears falling on the petals of roses, lilies, and carnations.

A pastor's wife spotted her from across the building and made her way over. The woman relieved her of the flowers, wrapped her arms around her and began praying. Time passed, and Alice wept in her arms, the stress and horror of the past week flowing out of her in those desperate tears.

A Town Called Sutherland Springs

After a while, when the tears began to slow, the woman asked Alice what was wrong.

All week long, Alice had been at the community center from early in the morning until after midnight, only to go home and collapse into bed before starting the process all over again. Alice and her husband, Oscar, had received donations from all over the community. People showed up with food trucks and barbeque grills, and cooked food for first responders and mourners alike. The community building was set up with cots and pallets for weary officers and first responders to try and catch a few hours of sleep amidst the nightmare that was this week.

In that week, Alice had helped organize a massive memorial at the baseball field. Churches from San Antonio brought equipment and worship bands. Whataburger and H-E-B donated food and tents. Crowds gathered to pray, and sing, and mourn. All the while, the community turned to Alice for help.

Alice explained to the pastor's wife how hopelessly lost she felt. She told her how badly she wanted to be useful in this situation. She explained to her all of the things which had happened in the last week, with the memorials, the vigil, and the makeshift living quarters for the responders. She told her how overwhelmed she felt and how she didn't know what to do.

The Pastor's wife was quiet for a time as Alice poured out all her anxieties and perceived shortcomings. When she was finished, the woman squeezed her tightly.

"Don't you understand, Alice?" she asked. "You have been telling me this whole time that you want to minister to the hurting, that you want to do God's work. And then you told me how much you have done this week, and how many people you have helped. Don't you understand, God has been using you this whole time to help this community?"

Her words penetrated through Alice's grief and helplessness. They made their way past her tears and began to clear the thick fog which had gripped Alice's mind. It was then that she began to realize that every time they needed something, it was God who had provided for them. It was God who sustained her and gave her the energy and ability to accomplish so much. Whenever Alice needed anything, whether it was a tent for the memorial service, DJ equipment for the worship team, or chairs, it seemed as if the need would be miraculously filled. Whenever the Texas Rangers, the Salvation Army, or the Secret Service required something of them, they just found it, lying around in wait. Now, the knowledge seemed so obvious and simple. But it was a revelation to her.

Alice sat there for some time, with the Pastor's wife speaking to her quietly and holding her hand. God had provided her all the tools necessary to do His work.

When she left, quite a while later, Alice knew that this wasn't the end of her ministry. It was merely the beginning. God had provided for her and her community thus far. If she trusted in Him further, who knows what else He could accomplish?

* * *

A Town Called Sutherland Springs

In the days following the shooting, Ryland Ward was in a medically induced coma. His injuries were so extensive that he had to undergo multiple surgeries and often had open wounds which couldn't be closed for days. During his trip to the hospital, and in the emergency room, Ryland died on the table more than once. The doctors and paramedics refused to give up on him, however, and continued to bring him back over and over again.

When the doctors pulled him out of the coma after a few days, his father was waiting anxiously at his side. The little boy's eyes opened wearily; eyelids heavy with a trauma which no little boy should have to endure. He was connected to machines which monitored his heart, his vitals, and his oxygen. They beeped rhythmically, the only noise in the otherwise quiet hospital. The sterile room around him was foreign and clinical. His dad, weary and burdened with grief, reached out and squeezed his hand.

"Ryland, can you hear me, buddy?" Chris asked, his voice cracking with an overflow of emotion.

Ryland's eyes struggled to focus. He took a deep breath and flexed his tiny hand within his father's.

"I saw God," Ryland said, his voice cracking from disuse. "He told me it wasn't my time yet. He told me I had to come home and take care of my daddy."

Ryland's words brought tears to the eyes of those present.

Later, Ryland's grandmother, Sandy, would ask him about what he saw. She wondered how he knew his sisters had passed away without being told. She wondered how the child didn't struggle with the anger and fear which plagued the rest of her family. Ryland told her he saw Jesus, holding his sisters' hands. He watched them enter Heaven together, with his stepmother Joann. That image, of little Brooke and Emily holding the hands of Christ as they entered Heaven, brought great comfort to Sandy and her family.

✳ ✳ ✳

In the week following the tragedy, Rusty Duncan barely slept. He spent most of his time at the church. He helped move the fallen victims and clean up the church building. He and his colleagues made themselves available to help in any way possible. One image haunted Rusty's mind: that little boy, clinging to life, flying away in the helicopter. Rusty watched the news for information about him. He read newspapers which reported on the casualties. He searched for the little boy's name, and always breathed a sigh of relief when he didn't see it. Finally, calls were made, and Rusty was put in contact with the Ward family.

When he walked into the hospital room where Ryland was recovering from countless surgeries, and awaiting many more, the tension in his chest released a bit.

He was so small in the hospital bed. His slight form looked so weak and pale amidst the machines and tubes which ran in a maze across his tiny body. But when he saw Rusty, he smiled.

"Do you know who I am?" Rusty asked the boy, not knowing what response he hoped for.

A Town Called Sutherland Springs

"I do," the little boy responded, his voice soft. "You yelled at me."

Rusty smiled. "Sorry about that."

From that moment, Rusty knew he was not done helping this little boy. Every Sunday, he visited the boy in the hospital, looking through the hundreds of cards which poured in from all over the world. He told stories and talked with the boy as he played with new toys. No matter how much pain Ryland was in, he never showed it. His bravery and strength helped Rusty sort through his own lingering emotions and trauma from what he saw that day.

Besides, if a little boy who had lost so much and been hurt so badly could still smile and laugh, how could he not himself?

One day, Rusty pushed Ryland's wheelchair into the lobby of the hospital to look at the giant, decorated Christmas tree.

"Do you have a fire truck?" Ryland asked him, the light from the Christmas tree sparkling in his bright eyes.

"Yes," Rusty responded. "Do you want to see it?"

Ryland smiled in excitement, sitting up a little straighter in his wheelchair. "Right now?" He asked. "Let's go take a ride in it right now!"

Rusty laughed. "I don't have it with me."

"Well, go get it!"

"I can't yet. But I tell you what, when the doctors say you can leave, I'll pick you up in it."

Karla Holcombe was a faithful woman. Her smile was constant, and her prayers meaningful. When the church began looking to expand, they considered buying the property next door. It used to be the old post office, until it was torn down. They loved their old chapel, as it had so much history to it, and many had come to Christ right there within its walls. With age, however, came many structural problems which were beginning to spiral out of control. The problem was the property next door was right on Highway 87 and was much too expensive for the humble country church to afford.

That did not stop Karla from praying.

For years, she could be seen wandering the edges of the property, Bible in hand and praying softly. She'd go every Sunday and Thursday, and occasionally even on Tuesdays. She would walk the border of the empty lot day after day, lifting requests for God to provide a miracle.

"Karla, we aren't going to be able to afford that property," people would tell her.

In response, Karla would offer a secret smile. "I'm not asking God to lower the price," she would say. "I am asking God to give us the property. You never know. We serve a big God."

After years of praying, Karla passed into Heaven in the church she loved, kneeling at its altar. Karla's spirit of faith, however, persisted. After the heartbreak, tears, funerals, and prayers, the church family received some surprising news. The next-door property, the empty lot where Karla had spent years walking, and praying over in earnest, had been donated, gifted to the church for a new chapel. This gift, wrought from Karla's prayers, comforted, and amazed the church family, even through the tragedy.

As they broke ground on the church months later, they knew Karla was by God's side, smiling down at them. It was like a parting gift to her family.

After all, the church serves a big God.

* * *

That December, shortly before Christmas, a group of churchgoers gathered as the sun began to set. They settled into the back of a flatbed trailer, bundled up and holding candles. Although everyone in the group was keenly aware of the missing members, they didn't feel alone. It was as if the fallen members of their church family were with them in spirit. That brought comfort to them as the truck began to pull the trailer through the streets of Sutherland Springs, guided by the spinning lights of a fire truck.

The church family sang Christmas carols. *Silent Night, Joy to the World, O Come all Ye Faithful*- the imperfect and beautiful notes of the songs drifting through the otherwise silent, sleepy, little town. Neighbors left their houses to listen as the trailer drove by, pulling congregants whose joy danced in their eyes with the candlelight, even through their pain.

When they passed by our house, the lights drove us outside. When I stepped out, onto the porch, I was greeted with cheerful waves and broad smiles. Barefoot, my wife and I walked into the yard, across the cold ground to the street where the caravan halted. The singing continued as members of the church hopped down from the trailer and embraced me and Pam. I added my own tone-deaf voice to the tune.

Surrounded by our new family, donning Santa hats, flashing Christmas light necklaces, and carrying burning candles, we sang with the friends whose grief we shared. The hope was contagious.

As the closing notes of *Joy to the World* echoed through 5th street, final hugs were given and the congregants climbed back into the trailer, continuing their journey as we walked back inside. As I shut the door behind me, the lights of the fire truck and the notes of the music fading, tears glistened in my eyes.

For the first time in what felt like a lifetime, I felt my heart beginning to knit back together. In the perfectly imperfect voice of the church, and in that song, I saw the shining hope of God.

✲ ✲ ✲

Ryland spent two months in the hospital. He underwent multiple surgeries to stitch his little body back together. After two months of surgeries, therapy, and painful recovery, Ryland received good news: he was going home.

Rusty kept his promise. On January 11, 2018, he brought his fire truck up to University Hospital in San Antonio, followed by a parade of other vehicles. Police officers in cars and motorcycles, EMS in other fire trucks, and even helicopters escorted the little boy from the hospital. People lined the streets and crowded bridges with signs, welcoming the little warrior back. Neighbors cheered and whistled as the parade of cars rode past, the sirens representing triumph this time, instead of pain.

All the while, the little boy beamed. He wanted to go faster; he wanted the sirens to be louder. He wanted Rusty to honk the horn more as he laughed and waved out the window. The escort that took him home would have befit a U.S. President. Ryland- who had spent Thanksgiving, Christmas, and his birthday in the hospital, was finally receiving the hero's homecoming he deserved.

After all, the little boy was a miracle. He consistently astounded the doctors and medical professionals who met him. The very fact that he was alive should have been impossible, save for a God who was not finished with his story and a volunteer firefighter who refused to let him go.

* * *

Five months after the tragedy, I stood among a crowd of people. My eldest daughter, Stephanie, stood before me. She was a stunning vision of lace, delicate flowers, and a smile so wide and beautiful that it was contagious. Her bright eyes glittered with an overwhelming happiness as her husband, Bruce, slipped his arm around her waist. He looked sharp today, clad in a navy-blue suit and a silver bow tie. Although his thick, red mustache and beard hid his mouth, it was evident by looking at him that he was smiling. His eyes were creased and joyful, his shoulders relaxed.

It was their wedding day. Moments before, they had stood together under a gazebo draped in flowers and gauzy tulle. In front of their friends, family, and God, they pledged to spend their lives together, for better or for worse. Bruce was now an official part of our family, although he had been an unofficial member for quite some time now.

The wedding was beautiful. It was filled with joy, laughter, and hope. The day was perfect and clear, and the love which the newlyweds shared for each other was evident to all those in attendance.

My family needed this day. I tried to keep mostly out of the limelight as we worked to sort through our emotions and heal from the trauma of that fateful day. I couldn't avoid it entirely, though. The story of Sutherland Springs had reached people all over the world. At home, I kept a box filled with letters from strangers. No one knew my address- they simply sent it to Stephen Willeford, Sutherland Springs. The postmaster knew in which box they belonged. It was overwhelming. People from across the world wrote to me, to thank me for what I did, and to let me know they were praying for my community. My family and I knew it was these prayers that carried us through the darkness we witnessed.

I still didn't see what I did as anything remarkable but continued to feel humbled as politicians and heroes from across the nation reached out to honor me. I had been asked to tell my story before crowds of people, which I agreed to do for two reasons: to warn others to be prepared, and to remind them that God should receive all the glory. I knew it was God that day who had called me, had strengthened my actions, hardened my nerves, and guided my shots. Since that day, I had felt a responsibility to tell the world.

A Town Called Sutherland Springs

Before me, Stephanie sat down on a folding chair in front of the crowd for the garter toss. When Bruce lifted her voluminous skirt, he saw the gun placed snugly in her embroidered cowgirl boot.

I had bought him a Ruger GT100, 7 shot .357 magnum, with a 6-inch barrel. Bruce had always loved revolvers, and this gun was one of his favorites. Bruce beamed as he pulled the gift from his new wife's boot. It was a Willeford family tradition that started when Rachel married Matt. A man protected his family, and for their union, I gave the new family the means to do so.

At Rachel's wedding, it had been a big surprise. The garter we ordered was a custom-fit holster. Matt's confused and surprised face had been priceless: as priceless as the laughter of the onlooking crowd. It was less of a surprise at Blake and Heather's wedding, two years later. The gun wasn't in the garter, but I gathered the crowd of friends and family to present the newlyweds a Springfield EMP. Blake had even helped me pick out the gun they wanted.

For Stephanie's wedding, everyone knew it was coming. The spectacle of the gun presentation at the previous weddings was practically legendary now. But that didn't lessen Bruce's excitement as he handled the firearm gingerly, respectfully. I stepped forward as the crowd laughed, approaching my new son-in-law to show him how to check if it was loaded. Of course, it wasn't, but Bruce already knew to check as a matter of safety.

"If we catch the garter, do we get the gun?" someone in the crowd yelled.

I had had a talk with Bruce as I was giving Stephanie away. I explained to him that a man protected his family, shielded them from harm, and led them closer to God. I explained to Bruce that I was handing over one of the most precious things in the world to me, and it was now his responsibility to protect and care for Stephanie.

Although the words had been true when I had told Matt the same thing, over four years earlier, they seemed to have heavier meaning in light of November 5th. So did the presentation of the gun. Before, the sentiment was just a closely held belief in the role of a man in the family. It was passing down a piece of advice and manhood to the next generation of guardians. Now, in the wake of November, it was as if I was passing down a promise.

I have always said I don't own any weapons. I only own firearms. Firearms become weapons only if used to do damage to another human being. I guess I have one now.

Days after the tragedy, news came out that the murderer had taken his own life at the scene of the wreck. But I had still shot the man six times. All but two of the bullets were deflected by his armor, but each one had made an impact. He felt them. It turned his fight into flight. Although the bullets did not ultimately kill him, my actions weighed heavily on my heart.

I never expected to be who I was now- hailed a hero, a man who has shaken hands with the President and Vice President of the United States, and a personal friend of a sitting US Senator. But here I was, and I know I can't take this responsibility lightly.

A Town Called Sutherland Springs

As the wedding festivities continued around me, I melted back into the crowd. Pam joined me by the wall of the reception hall. She looked beautiful that day, which wasn't at all surprising. Pam was the most beautiful woman in the world. She had stood by me, comforted me, and prayed for me. She was a godly wife and a wonderful mother. I feel so blessed to have her in my life.

Together, we sat on the white chairs which lined the walls of the hall, as the dancing began. We watched as Stephanie and Bruce took to the dance floor, their eyes only on each other. Stephanie laughed at something her husband said as he wrapped his arms around her. Their faces were close together and their eyes sparkled with love for each other.

In the corner, Matt, Rachel, Blake, and Heather stood together, watching, and talking amongst themselves.

Rachel was eight months pregnant now. They were expecting their girl in May. The day couldn't come soon enough for them. They were both ready to be parents, and ready to hold their little girl in their arms.

Little Alice Moira was a long-awaited treasure. She would be named after characters from some of Rachel's favorite books: Alice for a headstrong curiosity, Moira for a loving and gentle nature.

Matt and Rachel's house was finished now. They had been living in it for about a month. Although it was small, they had built it with their own hands and were incredibly proud of the fruits of their labor. The house was set up, the crib put together, and the baby onesies folded and organized. Now, all there was to do was wait.

Blake and Heather had recently announced they were expecting a child as well. She wasn't due until October, but she and Blake were thrilled. They planned to build a home on my family land, where they could raise their child in the town they loved.

I couldn't believe all of our children, including Stephanie and her new husband, planned to build out on our land- the same land on which I was raised. Even though the last few months had been incredibly hard for all of us, it had cemented our relationships and made us even closer to each other. For that, we all felt incredibly blessed.

Stephanie's eyes searched for me as the newlywed's first dance ended and it came time for our own dance. Tears pricked at my eyes as I heard the notes of an old lullaby I used to sing to rock Stephanie to sleep. Stephanie's own voice was recorded singing the lyrics as a friend played the guitar. I held my daughter closer, my hands tightly gripping hers, swaying gently to the beautiful music.

My family definitely needed this day. We needed to be surrounded by love, laughter, and the hope which a new marriage brought. I hadn't realized how badly I needed that until I was there, surrounded by friends, family, and loved ones, swaying on the dance floor, and holding my beautiful, smiling daughter.

With her hands in mine, I wept grateful, happy tears.

✷ ✷ ✷

Months later, Sarah Slavin attended a ladies' conference with the women of First Baptist Church. She was

A Town Called Sutherland Springs

still trying to put her life back together. She had lost not only her mother and father, but her brother, nieces and nephews, sister-in-law, and dear friends. Their absence left a gnawing hole in her heart – a hole whose ragged edges ached terribly. She was doing her best to keep it together, especially for her daughter's sake. Some days were easier.

Since her experience with God in the car on the morning of the tragedy, Sarah had developed a deeper relationship with Him than she had ever before known. The words which he had spoken to her that morning were true- although the grief was heavy, and her little girl missed her lost family members, God had provided for Elene during Sarah's grief in a way which was miraculous. She knew she didn't need to worry about her anymore.

Sarah also had a renewed outlook on life. Now, worship songs often brought her to tears, and she found herself taking the same delight and gratitude in the beauty of the sunset which her mother always had. Although her relationship with God had deepened and grown, Sarah sometimes still felt like she was spinning her wheels too fast and getting nowhere. Just when she thought she was going to be ok, another memory of her family or the longing to hear her mother's laugh would send her spiraling into grief again. This weekend was a welcome retreat.

The speaker at the ladies' conference kept preaching about being *'Undone'*. This phrase triggered a song in Sarah's head, blaring through her thoughts and playing in a loop. It was called Undone by Weezer. She couldn't figure out why this song wouldn't leave her alone.

During her prayers, the song was an overlay in the back of her head. Occasionally, during conversations with other ladies or at meals, Sarah would unwittingly find herself humming it and having difficulty focusing on her surroundings. The chorus blared as she was trying to sleep, as she was brushing her teeth, and as she walked to the conference.

If you want to destroy my sweater, pull this thread as I walk away ... watch me unravel ... I've come undone.

The song was the worst kind of ear worm- it stole her focus and haunted her. It got so bad she found herself trying to pray it away, begging God to make it stop. She tried singing other songs, trying to focus on different lyrics, but the words of this song continued to weave into every thought. Eventually, she would circle back to it, only to have to start the process all over again. Nothing worked.

The song only got louder.

Ok, God, she jokingly conceded. *If there is a point to this forsaken song looping in my head, please make it clear. I'm tired of this.*

During a break between lessons, a memory app on Sarah's phone pinged. She glanced at her phone and saw a picture she had taken two years before to the day. For the first time since the conference started, the song which was punishingly repeating in her brain stopped. Sarah smiled at the memory, closed her eyes, and let herself fade into the past for a moment.

They were in her father's shop. He owned his own company called American Canvas Works. He did custom canvas work- anything from awnings to covers, including the occasional car upholstery. He was best known for his cattle trailer tarps. Bryan made the products, and Karla handled the books.

Recently, Sarah had begun helping her father. This particular day, he was teaching her how to make a tarp for a cattle trailer. While Elene and Noah played in the pen nearby, their soft giggles and babbles providing adorable background music, Bryan patiently and skillfully taught Sarah each step involved in crafting the cattle tarp. Sarah smiled as she remembered his rough, strong hands handling the thick material. The memory of his familiar, warm voice and off-kilter sense of humor brought tears to her eyes as she ached to be with him.

The process of crafting the tarp was long and laborious, especially for Sarah. When one of the last steps came, she was relieved. One of the only things left to do was to sew the ends together with the sewing machine. This, Sarah could do. Bryan had walked her through all the other steps, but this was a simple, straight seam. She was no stranger to a sewing machine. Over the years, she had become an expert: she knew how to make quilts and had been sewing automotive upholstery for years now. She told her dad she could handle this part, and confidently approached the machine as he stepped away to work on another project. Sarah measured the two pieces, lined them up perfectly, and added some midway marks to keep her in check. Then, she began sewing.

When she reached the end of the seam, the ends did not meet. They were off by about a quarter of an inch. She sat back, confused. She examined the seam, wondering where she went wrong. In a cattle tarp, a quarter of an inch was a big deal. If it was just a little bit off, it would be painfully obvious in the end, and it wouldn't fit. Frustrated, Sarah snatched up a seam ripper, and began undoing the seam to start over. She wouldn't get it wrong again. She could do this. She had done this before. It was simple, right?

As she reached the end of the second seam, she was again frustrated to discover that her measurements had been off. Once again, the ends of the tarp did not meet. Sarah didn't understand. This was just sewing, and she knew how to sew. She hauled the material off the sewing machine again, placing the thick, heavy canvas in her lap and examining the seams once more. Where had she gone wrong?

Again, Sarah undid her seam. She started over, re-measuring, adding more midway marks, hauling the material back and forth, and trying to double and triple check her marks. When she completed the seam once more, it still didn't match. At this point, Sarah was getting incredibly frustrated. The material was heavy, and thick. It was a tightly woven polyester canvas coated in a thick layer of vinyl. Maybe it was the material. It was heavier, with less give than anything she had worked with before. Maybe that was the problem. Sarah mustered up her courage and tried again.

When she reached the end of the seam, and saw the uneven ends, she felt like screaming. Finally, she was ready to give up. She called her dad over, the frustration clear in her voice.

"What am I doing wrong?" she asked, exasperated. "I don't understand, I know how to sew!"

A Town Called Sutherland Springs

Bryan took it from her, with his signature smile.

"You're not holding your mouth right," he responded.

Sarah watched her father sit down at the machine, his skillful hands running across the fabric with familiarity. She watched him push the pedal and heard the loud, rhythmic shutter of the sewing machine drowning out the giggles of the girls nearby. In a quarter of the time, Bryan straightened and showed her the seam. It was perfect, which frustrated Sarah even further.

"I don't understand!" Sarah exclaimed, shifting the perfect seam through her hands. "You did exactly what I did. Why didn't it work?"

Her father's smile shone clear and bright. "You're not the master," he responded simply. "You should have come to me sooner for help. Since you tried so many times, there are all these holes in the seam which didn't need to be here. You did three times the amount of work and didn't get very far. I could have helped you put it together sooner."

Sarah sighed at the sound of his voice, the twinkle in his eyes, the memory of him. That is how she felt. Like she was doing all this work, only to stand in the same place. Like her wheels were spinning and spinning, trying to get out of thick mud which only pulled her down deeper the more she tried to escape.

I've come UNDONE ... the lyrics of the song screamed in her ear, so suddenly it startled her.

Sarah's eyes snapped open. Undone. That is exactly what had happened to her. She had come completely undone, like the slow unraveling of a sweater.

"You're not the Master," she heard her dad say again.

Sarah realized that this whole time, even though she knew she should have been relying on God to get her through her grief, she had been relying on herself. She had been sitting at a sewing machine, pushing on the pedals, measuring her life, and putting down marks where she was sure she could bind herself back together. She had been hauling all that weight by herself and coming up short every time. The ends weren't meeting, and now she was undone and riddled with holes. All this time, she should have turned to the Master. He could have helped her a long time ago, before she got to this broken, unraveled state.

Tears pricked her eyes as she smiled, knowing that God and her father were watching out for her. She brushed the tears away as the break ended, and she followed the crowd of people toward the next sermon. The lyrics of the song finally dissipated and scattered in her head, leaving her in peace.

When she got home, the memories of her family felt different. Although her heart still ached at their absence, she felt a little lighter, as if the burden of her grief had been lifted and placed on much broader shoulders. It was easier now to walk through the past and enjoy the memories of her family.

During one of these trips, Sarah found an old picture of Elene and Noah. Elene and Noah were best friends. They had spent many hours together in the baby "jail" playpen in Mor Mor and Grumpy's shop. They had crawled and run around the house with flashing toys and Cabbage Patch dolls. Once, when they discovered a large cardboard box, they played for hours, their childlike imaginations running away and taking them on grand adventures. Sarah snapped a picture of the moment – a picture which she still cherishes. When she rediscovered the delightful moment, she shared the memory with her daughter, who was now four.

"Oh, Noey," Elene cooed. "I love her little face."

"Do you remember this, love?" Sarah asked, allowing herself the bittersweet moment of grief which follows the loss of a loved one.

Elene nodded and looked up at her mother contemplatively. "Mama, do they have boxes in Heaven?"

"I don't know. Why, baby?"

"I just want to know if Noah has a box to play in now," her daughter responded matter-of-factly.

Later, Elene found a new box. With Sarah's help, she loaded her tiny newborn cousin, Brighton, into the box. Then they set off into space. The box was not mere cardboard and tape, after all, but a rocket ship, which Elene used to propel herself, and her new cousin, to fly it all the way to Heaven, so Noah could meet the newborn and have a box in which to play.

***

It was Christmastime, 2018. I sat on the couch in Matt and Rachel's living room, a tiny baby clutched in my arms. Charlotte, the youngest grandchild to join the Willeford family, watched me with large, watery, blue eyes filled with wonder and curiosity. Her soft, angelic voice cooed occasionally as I beamed at her, barely able to contain my excitement. She was barely two months old and had already stolen my heart.

Blake and Heather, Charlotte's parents, chatted good-naturedly while opening presents and cracking jokes. They were happy but tired – the kind of tired that only parents of newborns understood.

My wife sat next to me, Christmas presents in her lap as she wrestled a squirming and energetic 7-month-old. Alice giggled and burbled, her bright eyes sparkling. Her gummy, and still-toothless grin flashed often as she attempted to tear at Pam's presents and eat the paper. Holding on to the infant was a struggle. She was so full of life and so wonderfully curious that she simply didn't have the patience to sit still for even a moment. Pam laughed as she wrestled the child, the joy of the little girl wildly contagious to whomever witnessed it.

Stephanie and Bruce sat on the living room floor, leaning against the wall as Rachel continued to pass out the presents which were piled along the stairs. Matt sat across from the couch, munching on the breakfast tacos and monkey bread which Rachel had prepared, his eyes darting often to admire his little girl.

The tiny home was filled with laughter, and happy voices. Laughter at the jokes and jabs which the family threw at each other from across the room, laughter at the simple, hilarious gifts they received- gifts like toilet paper guns, and silly t-shirts, and laughter at the new noises and babbles from the tiny babies. There was so much relaxed happiness to be found in each other's presence. The events of the past year had brought us all closer together, and the arrival of the two precious girls had radically changed all our lives.

The truth was a lot of healing had been brought by the girls. The hope which new life brought was desperately needed after such tragedy. Alice and Charlotte were bright points of light in the dark tunnel of grief and confusion through which we struggled. Their joy and their innocence were needed to see the world with fresh eyes.

So much had happened in the last year. I had spoken at the NRA national convention, in front of thousands. I had a new son-in-law. I now had two of the most beautiful granddaughters the world had ever seen. My family was closer than ever before, bound together and made stronger by the tragedy we experienced. Also, we finally knew where we belonged. For a long time, we had searched for a church home. We had been floating from building to building, never quite fitting in, never quite settling. We hadn't even realized that our church family was waiting for us, just a few steps from our front door.

The new building was being built. It could be seen from any direction, rising above the town like a beacon of hope. The new church grounds would be open in May 2019. It would be beautiful, although nothing could be as beautiful as the people who attended.

I had met people whose strength astounded me- like the woman who lost her young daughter and husband, but still smiled, laughed, and played with the children at church. She smiled through the tears which often shone in her eyes.

I had met a young woman who lost most of her family, but still clung to God, knowing healing could be found in His arms.

I had met a man who was now bound to a wheelchair, but rejoiced in the power of his testimony.

I heard stories from the congregation – story after story of those who carried on, trusting God to carry them through such suffering, and such pain. I couldn't believe the strength of these people, and I felt so very blessed to be a part of their story.

Occasionally, I still struggle with the nightmares that November brought. Sometimes, I still struggle with the grief and the guilt of that terrible day. But now, looking around me, listening to the laughter of my kids, their spouses, and the beautiful cooing of my precious granddaughters, I knew we would pull through this.

This was my new normal now. It would never feel normal. The things I saw would always haunt the back of my mind, and I would be forever changed.

But I was beginning to understand how to adjust around it. And, with all these blessings, with all the good which surrounded us daily, how could I not?

A Town Called Sutherland Springs

Afterword

Many hours went into the writing of this book. We represented the facts as honestly and straightforwardly as we were able, after countless interviews with victims, witnesses, law enforcement, first responders, and family members. Although we only memorialize 23 victims, Sutherland Springs lost 26 beautiful souls that day. When writing this book, we strove to fairly represent each person. We have left out those whom we were not able to reach, or whose family requested that they be omitted. Their names can be found in public documents, and we hope the readers will help us make sure that these people are never forgotten.

We understand many will read this book hoping to get an insight into why the killer committed such a horrible act, and what led to the events described - but this was never going to be that kind of book. These suppositions and psychological studies can be made by other people. We know the truth of why these things happened. They were committed because evil attacked our church and our community. Evil sometimes defies explanation. There is no sense in senseless acts of violence, and no healing can be found in understanding the killer's motives. As you have now read, we did not even mention his name. The reason for this is simple: we hope that what is taken away from this testimony is the strength of the people in our town, not the evil of the man who committed these acts. He has had enough fame, and enough attention. We ask that you remember the names of those we lost, and those extraordinary people who banded together to save lives and comfort the hurting.

Don't forget their strength, and their fighting spirit. Don't forget their trust in God, and love for one another.

And please, don't forget the little town called Sutherland Springs.

About the Authors

Stephen Willeford

Stephen Willeford lived a quiet life in the town of Sutherland Springs until 2017, when a madman entered the First Baptist Church. Since the events of that day, Stephen has become an outspoken advocate for preparedness and gun rights. His experience and knowledge has taken him all across the United States, to speak with churches, politicians, and school boards, as well as Congress, and in State Houses. Currently, Stephen works for Gun Owners of America (GOA), as a National Spokesperson and Industry and Grassroots Liaison.

Rachel Howe

As the daughter of Stephen Willeford, Rachel Howe was trained and raised around firearms from an early age. After the events in November 2017, Rachel felt called to write this book as a testimony of the pain and faith of the community she loves. She is a writer and artist, living in Sutherland Springs, Texas, in a tiny home with her husband, Matt, and a small group of wild, country daughters.

A Town Called Sutherland Springs

Acknowledgments

In his book, *The Screwtape Letters*, C.S. Lewis wrote "*Courage is not simply one of the virtues but the form of every virtue at the testing point*". There were so many circumstances during the events of this book, and the writing of it, that tested every virtue imaginable. The courage that was displayed by those we spoke to was nothing short of inspiring. We want to thank all of those who had the courage to speak with us and relive what was easily one of the most traumatic experiences imaginable.

We want to thank the family members of those who lost their lives for sharing stories of their loved ones with us, so that they could be remembered for their strength, beauty, and faith.

We want to thank the first responders, law enforcement officials, and hospital workers, who worked hard to save lives that day, and in the days, months, and years that followed.

We want to thank our community, and the First Baptist Church of Sutherland Springs for their inspiring bravery, and faith, which has uplifted us, and encouraged us, when it seemed that darkness was overwhelming.

Stephen Willeford & Rachel Howe

Thank you to all those who helped make this book possible. For Pam Willeford, who sat for hours pouring over every word after Rachel had written it, making sure that the grammar was correct, and that her run on sentences did not get too out of control. This book would not have been possible without your constant support and love. Thank you for reading it, and re-reading it, even through the tears and the heartache. Your spirit is truly incredible.

Thank you to John Lott, who contacted Stephen when no publisher would seem to have us and helped us figure out the confusing world of self-publishing. Without you, who knows how long this book would have been stuck in limbo.

Thank you to all the media personalities, politicians, and podcast hosts who have continued to speak about our town, to make sure the true events of what happened that day are not forgotten.

Thank you to Gun Owners of America, for believing in this story, and encouraging us to pull it out of the depths of our computer, and pursue publishing again, even after many rejection letters.

Thank you to Daniel Contreras, from New Dirt Studios for the cover design, and the author photos. He is immensely talented, and we couldn't be more grateful. We also thank Nikki Goeser for suggesting the concept for the cover.

Most of all, we want to thank God. Sometimes, upon reflection, things that happened that day still seem too incredible and miraculous to believe. The community of Sutherland Springs saw God walking, even through immense

A Town Called Sutherland Springs

suffering. God did not leave us. He was there, holding us, guiding us, and leading us the entire time.

Evil did not win.

> *"When you pass through the waters, I will be with you; and through the rivers, they shall not overwhelm you; when you walk through fire you shall not be burned, and the flame shall not consume you." Isaiah 43:2, ESV*

Praise for A Town Called Sutherland Springs

"...Willeford's heroic and selfless intervention saved lives and demonstrated that a "good guy with a gun is the only thing that stops a bad guy with a gun." Willeford found himself thrust in the public eye for his actions, but he was simply a well-trained marksman who rose to the occasion when he was all that stood between the people of his community and death at the hands of a madman. His story is a reminder that the real heroes among us are sometimes our friends and neighbors who risk their own lives to protect ours."

—Mike Huckabee, host of the talk show Huckabee

"Stephen Willeford is an American hero in the same tradition of every hero in American history... ordinary people doing extraordinary things. His story is so much more than his heroic act on that dreadful day in 2017. It is the story of an American family and community that will give you hope for the future of a nation struggling to remember what made it so great in the first place. The values that gave Stephen the grit and courage to save so many lives that day are the same values that can rebuild our broken Nation. I thank God for Stephen and his story and his willingness to be a voice of hope for all of us."

— Rick Green, Founder of Patriot Academy

A Town Called Sutherland Springs

"This is an amazing book! So powerful. So tragic. It brought me to tears. It is a riveting account of courage and competence in the face of unspeakable horror. Every American must read and remember the story of A Town Called Sutherland Springs."

—Lt. Col. Dave Grossman, Author of On Killing, On Combat, On Spiritual Combat, and On Hunting

Made in the USA
Middletown, DE
17 April 2024